DAILY QUOTE
To Nourish Your Agile Soul
Book Three

By: Yudha Pratama

DAILY QUOTE: To Nourish Your Agile Soul - Book Three

Author's note: I intentionally omitted the Table of Contents in this book. You will just have to explore and see what nuggets and Easter eggs you will find. What Easter Eggs you asked? If you know it, you will know it when you see it.

Special thanks to Michael Bernstein. Without the countless hours we spent talking about agility, this book wouldn't be possible. And there is no word of gratitude I could say to express my appreciation for the great work done by Jessica Hurst, Kristi Desai & Jordan Gasc

Skyheart Publishing
Bellevue, WA 98005

Cover graphic design by Yudha Pratama

PREFACE

First thing first. There is no single original idea in this book. Everything that I say here I learned from others. I learned by reading the books they wrote, listening to their lectures on YouTube or Audible. Often, I am having hard time remembering which books or authors a certain idea that I talked about. In my mind, there are tidbits of knowledge that I find interesting. So, if you get to the point and you wonder "Did Yudha say this, or did he quote some famous people?" You won't go wrong in deciding that it must have been some famous people who said it.

Even the creation of this book is not an original idea. I was talking to Jess H., and she showed me her book "The Daily Stoic: 366 Meditations on Wisdom, Perseverance, and The Art of Living" and I thought, "hm, that's a good idea. I should emulate it and make a version that talks about agile, project management, product development and sometimes, just about being good human.

Someone else asked me why I was doing this. I told him that it wasn't an altruistic gesture. I enjoy talking about agility and if everyone is agile, my job will be so much easier.

The intent of this book is not to indoctrinate you with my beliefs. Think of the discussion as a discussion. Read the quote [it is the TL/DR of the page] and read my interpretation of the quote. There will be many ways to interpret them. There is no guarantee that my way will be better than your way. The point is to read it and reflect and hopefully, your reflection will nudge to continuously improve your people and processes.

I am not a Mandalorian. I don't believe in "this is the way!" – I believe that there are many ways. A better (but definitely less catchy) phrase is "this is a way" – you've seen my way, now, you go and try "your way!"

HOW THIS BOOK WAS CREATED

Someone asked if I created this book using Scrum. The answer "kind of."
He said, "what do you mean "kind of?" there is no "kind of" framework!"
I don't use Scrum because I am the Product Owner, Scrum Master,
Developer and QA. I still worked on 2 weeks sprints cadence.

I knew the key milestones that I need to hit. I knew that I have about
around 100 pages to write and have 4 Sprints to do it. That meant that I
need to finish 25 pages per Sprint or 2 pages per day. Although I didn't
use Jira, created kanban board or user story to organize the work, I had
visualized the end-to-end flow in my mind. Basically, I used Scrum
mindset to help me write the book, not the Scrum events or artifacts.

Although this is not my first time writing a book (I have written a book
entirely using Scrum framework before. A couple years ago, in my
Advanced Agile Project Management class at the Northeastern
University, my students and I wrote a book "Agile Adoption 101" purely
using Scrum – complete with Jira, User Story, kanban board, Daily Scrum
– and all the fixings), I still fall prey to one of the most common problems
in development. I still put the QA towards the end, instead of shifting
left and do QA as the writing goes. Suddenly I am in a mad scramble.
Consequently, I had to ask Jess, Kristi and Jordan to pull a couple of all-
nighters (along with their busy day job) to help make sure that there are
no glaring mistakes in the book. Thank you, Jess, Kristi and Jordan.

Had I shifted left early and performed the QA every time a day or chapter
is completed there wouldn't be any need for heroic to get this work
released on time.

A valuable lesson is learned!

*Note: I bounced ideas with Character.ai, consulted Wikipedia, scoured my book
collection and asked Google a lot in the process of writing this book. I learned that
character.ai sometimes make sh*t up – but it is still a good tool if you know how to
probe, ask follow-up questions and fact-check the answers.*

JULY

JULY 1

"Adopt the attitude that continuous planning is a good thing – In every iteration, expect your plans to change (albeit in small ways if your planning is effective). Don't fall into the trap of thinking that the plan is infallible."

- Ian Spence

Many people believe that we don't need to plan to agile. Isn't it said so in the Agile Manifesto, they said. Some would even quote the manifesto line that says: *"responding to change over following a plan."*

Of course, if they have actually read and understood the whole thing, instead of just grabbing some soundbites, they will realize that their statement was farthest from the truth, all the way to the other spectrum. As a matter of fact, in agile, there are a lot, and I mean, A LOT of plannings. For example, the Daily Scrum (or Daily Stand Up) is a planning event – where the team plan on what to accomplish for the day. This plan is a subset of a larger plan that they did at the beginning of every Sprint – during Sprint Planning. The plan during Sprint Planning may be a subset of a Release Plan and the Release Plan may be part of a Product Roadmap (which is also another plan.)

The key to planning in agile is that instead of planning based on a fixed event in the future, we plan at smaller increment and adjust our plans accordingly to the new information that we have learned. The most important part is the act of planning itself, not the plan. The act of planning forces us to be more deliberate in outlining our action and learnings from the feedback. Remember, planning is essential. The plans themselves, they are worthless. Take heed from Mike Tyson's warning "Everyone has a plan until they get punched in the mouth!"

JULY 2

Who doesn't like perfect requirements? No one. That's who. Anyone with the right mind would want perfect requirements.

There is only one teeny tiny problem with that, perfect requirements, almost always, do not exist in software development. It is one of the reasons why we prefer to use an iterative method (a.k.a. agile) as opposed to a predictive method (a.k.a. waterfall). In an iterative development method, we have agreed that we couldn't accurately predict the future, so we take a few small steps at a time, try as much as we can to peek around the corner, adjust and iterate and do it all over again until we get to the desired destination.

A word of caution – bloatware. Just because you can build it, it doesn't mean that you should. You should try to avoid building your product for *everyone*. Have a specific customer or segment in mind and fulfill the need well. Often, your most valuable customers only use about 20% of the features that you build. Take away the remaining 80%. Better still, reframe that 80% for different segment of your users and see which 20% those new segment uses and so on. This method is known as the 80/20 Principle (or the Pareto Principle named after its progenitor, Vilfredo Pareto)

As an avid gardener, Italian engineer and economist, Pareto observed that around 20% of his pea plants produce 80% of the total yield and he wondered if the same phenomena applied somewhere else. He found that 80% of the wealth was owned by only 20% of the population. The principle has been found to apply to almost everything.

JULY 3

"I have six honest serving friends (they taught me all I knew); Their names are What and Why and When. And How, and Where and Who."

- Rudyard Kipling

The method of asking for the What, Why, When, How, Where and Who is known as the "Kipling Method" taken from a poem written by Rudyard Kipling.

This method is very useful in product development, software development or general personal development. In creating a product one-pager or product requirements document, for example, you will find out that it generally tries to determine *why* we are building the product, *what* the product is about, *who* are customers are, *how* is our product is different from another product, *when* do we plan to release the product (market rhythm) and *where* (or which platform, market or segment) we are aiming. This method is especially power when used in performing a root cause analysis (RCA). Using this can help us systematically narrow down the problem, identify the underlying cause, which can lead to a more effective and lasting solution. And in the spirit of kaizen, this practice can help foster a culture of learning, a culture of continuous improvement in our organization.

Taiichi Ohno said that the practice of asking why – five times was adapted from Sakichi Toyoda (the founder of Toyota Industry Corporation) habit of watching how things work and asking why. This method is so integral, Ohno said that it is the "basis of Toyota scientific approach" whenever they find a problem.

JULY 4

"You are never as good as you look when you win. And you are never as bad as you look when you lose."

- Lou Holtz

Let me just come out and say it. "Life is not fair!" If you don't believe me, open the Bible – Matthew 25:29: "For unto every one that hath shall be given, and he shall have abundance: but from him that hath not shall be taken away even that which he hath." This is commonly referred to as "the Matthew Effect."

It has turned out that we, as human being, are full of biases, rule-of-thumb and pre-conditions. We have a collection of mental models that we use to get us through the day. (The reasons? It's because thinking is a very taxing act, so our brains create build many shortcuts so that we think as little as possible). When we see someone who has just completed a successful project, we tend to assign positive feeling towards the person. This is known as the "halo effect," and when someone was not successful, we tend to assign negative feelings, and this is called the "horn effect."

An example of the latest Apple Magic Mouse. Do you see where the charging port is located? It's one of the dumbest product designs, ever. No product manager in the right mind would think that it is a good idea to put the charging port there. Unless you are an Apple fanboy. A friend of mine, who is a total fanboy, told me that it's intentional. The battery last very long anyway and you should have more than one Magic Mouse to alternate the use. Because Apple invented the iPod and iPhone, to many, Apple can do no wrong. That is an example of a halo effect in action.

We are wise to heed Lou Holtz's observation to view a person's capability as it is. Don't be too harsh on some failings or overtly swooned by past success.

JULY 5

"Solomon Paradox: People's tendency to reason more wisely about other people's problems than their very own."

- Igor Grossmann

You probably have heard of the "Judgment of Solomon" – where two women claimed to be the mother of a child. Solomon resolved it by offering to cut the child in two and shared them between the two. One woman decided to spare the child and renounced her claim. Solomon decided to give the child to that woman. This famous story aside. Solomon often considered not as wise as the story made him out to be.

The point is to take any advice (solicited or unsolicited) with a grain of salt. I am sure that everyone that takes the effort to give advice, means well. It just that it may not always applicable to your situation.

Companies who hired consultant need to be weary of the Solomon Paradox. Although they are often useful is providing an outside view, they often lack the long-term commitment that are required for true success. Consultants have the habit of applying some predetermined solutions (that had worked previously in their experience.) Consultants also often 'find" problems that they just happened to have the solutions for. This phenomena is known as the "Shirky Principle" that states "institution will try to preserve the problems to which they are the solution."

The best course of action (warning – this is also some advice!) is to evaluate your situation, evaluate the advice and see if it can work for you. Whenever possible, try it (as an experiment), have as little commitment as possible. In product development parlance, build an MVP of the solutions and see if it works.

JULY 6

"The Law of Diminishing Intent: The longer you wait to do something you should do now, the greater the odds that you will never actually do it."

- Jim Rohn

John Kotter, the famous change management guru, in his book "The Heart of Change" retold a story from a Ron Marshall with the title "The Body in the Living Room"

The realtor told Ron "This is a fixer-upper, a real fixer-upper, a sixty-five-year-old house. Now, you've got to make sure that you make a list of all the things that you wanted to get fixed, and get it done in the first six months!" … "because after six months, you get used to it. It seems to fit. You get used to stepping over the dead body in the living room." Yikes! (Yes, this is a metaphor. I wonder about the smell. But maybe, we get used to the stink too!)

This phenomenon is related the Students Syndrome where people tend to procrastinate until last minute to do something (we tend to avoid work) or Parkinson Effect the tendency to expand work to fill the available time (we tend stretch work if we have long deadline).

The same principle applies to any change (improvement) efforts. When we see something that can and should be improved, we start doing something about it. Make it a priority. The more we put up with it, the more it will become acceptable and before we know it, we will find ourselves saying "That's the way we do things here! We don't need your stinkin', brand-spankin' different way of doing it!" The key to successful change initiative is to do it now, and to have short(er) deadline.

JULY 7

"Drop by drop is the water pot filled. Likewise, the wise man, gathering it little by little, fills himself with good."
- The Buddha

Maybe I can be so bold as to rephrase the quote above with *"Iteration by iteration is the product built. Wise developers releasing small features every Sprints, builds good solution." – The Yoda*

Once upon a time, a long, long time ago, before Y2K (that is year 2000 for those young whipper snappers who never had to face the fear of Armageddon caused by software developers) software was released in a "big bang" method. The customer peered into the future, decided what the customer should want, wrote detailed requirements, gave them to the developers. The developers locked themselves in a basement (sometimes, with a small window, most of the time only with some potted plants for company) typed furiously, fueled by gallons and gallons of Mountain Dew, emerge one or two years later with the finished product, on spec, only to find out that the world or market has moved on. This process has been pejoratively called the "waterfall process." Waterfall can be beautiful. If you are building something that the result is known, waterfall process is great, but it wasn't so great for new innovative software project.

Iterative software development (agile) was born in response to the uncertainties inherent in many innovative software developments. In agile, we build product or solutions like creating a scaffolding. Little by little. Build just enough, an MVP – Most Viable Product, to see if there is a market for it. Some would build an MMF – Most Marketable Feature, there is a difference, but the principle is the same. Do it bit by bit. Continuously built upon what you have validated, obtain feedback, adapt and iterate.

JULY 8

"Specifications will never be fully understood."

- Ziv's Law

Building an MVP sounds so much easier conceptually than in practice. Everyone has an idea what an MVP is. How minimum is "minimum?"

There is no easy answer to this – and the best the answer is "it depends." It depends on the state of the market your product is entering. If you are building an MVP for an electric car, it must have everything that is expected of what a regular car should be plus your differentiating features. If you are building something that hasn't existed before (like when Steve Jobs introduced the iPad) the specifications will be different.

You can use the Kano Model to help gauge what the minimum could be. The Kano model is a theory for product development and customer satisfaction developed by Noriaki Kano, which classifies customer preferences into five categories and three key attributes. The attributes are: Dissatisfiers (missing the basic needs), Satisfiers (meeting the basic needs) and Delighters (exceeding the basic need expectations). A good minimum must fulfill all the satisfiers requirements and have some (more is better) delighters requirements.

This model is very useful in providing framework for understanding customer requirements and needs. It can used in product development marketing and operations. The same model can also be applied to theory of motivation (see Herzberg Hygiene Theory discussion in later date, You will find that Herzberg theory is similar to the Kano Model.

JULY 9

I've never really liked the term "sprint" in agile. Every time I hear that term, I feel exhausted. In sport, sprinting means running over a short distance at the top-most speed within a limited period.

As a matter of fact, Jeff Sutherland, the co-creator of Scrum, intended the sprint to be short, intense period of focus and stop and evaluate where we are. The problem is that most practitioners don't stop to evaluate. The sprints have become a brief period in a marathon. I personally like the term iteration better because it evokes the feeling of addition and learning.

Anyway, in agile we work in a timeboxed period of 1-to-4-week sprints. At the end of sprint, the team evaluate their sprint burndown to see how well they execute their sprint plan. Raul C. is one of the masters of great execution of his teams' plan. It is folly to expect to go according to plan (thus expecting to see smooth burndown in the chart.). The reality of software development is that things are unpredictable, predictions (such as story point estimations) are doubly so. So, don't look at the sprint burndown as the goalpost. Instead look at how the team is achieving the sprint goal instead. Somedays, the burndown will look uglier and someday, not so.

Even though the suggested timebox is 1-to-4-week, most companies have 2-week Sprints. The length of the Sprint is largely determined by what I call, the rate of change to your product. If the rate of change is slow, you can get away with even a 4-week Sprint. If the rate of change is very fast, we may want to try a 1-week Sprint.

JULY 10

"Narrative transforms an insignificant object into a significant one."

- Rob Walker

A few years ago, I took the Verde Canyon train tour near Sedona, AZ. It was an easy and relaxing train ride that ended in a dilapidated old shack. No one paid much attention to the shack until the tour guide started telling us about the shack. The tour guide told us that this shack was the train station featured in an old western classic "How The West Was Won." Immediately after that, everyone, yes, me included, started taking pictures of that dilapidated old shack. The narrative provided by the tour guide has transformed a dilapidated old shack into a memorable landmark.

We do the same thing when we use user stories in our work to capture requirements. People used to write reams and reams of requirements and they are seldom accurate. Requirements also confine creativities. We use user stories to capture requirements in the form of intent. User stories provided the why and the what. The developers then have the freedom to use their creativity and expertise to achieve the how.

Jonathan Haidt said that "the human is a story processor, not a logic processor." it is much easier for people to remember and understand stories than a list of requirements. Our ancestors had been telling stories since the learned that they can etch cave walls. It is from their storytelling effort that they passed on everything that they learned for survival. It is from their storytelling that they created a foundation of learning-animal – one of the traits that eventually separated us from other mammals or the rest of the animal kingdoms.

JULY 11

"I didn't have time to write a short letter, so I wrote a long one instead."

- Mark Twain

Some of you who are used to getting detailed requirements handed to you may find the use of user stories as a proxy for requirements, inadequate. How could a simple statement of "as a [user], I want to [do something], so that [benefit], can replace those reams of reams of requirements.

The problem with those reams and reams of requirement is that they are lengthy not because they are thorough. Most of them may actually contain less information and full of useless boilerplate content that does not add value. People often waste time separating the wheat from the chaff because the creator of the requirements document does not spend the necessary effort to fully understand what's truly needed and what's not.

Writing a good user story requires the writer to understand the who, the what and the why and to be able to express those key components as concisely as possible. It takes a lot of forethought and deliberation to be concise.

Good User Story follows a simple criterion that form INVEST acronym, they are:
- I – Independent; can be completed independent of other story.
- N – Negotiable; it's not a fixed state, can be further broken down.
- V – Valuable; there must be value to the customers.
- E – Estimable; developer have enough information to estimate.
- S – Small; can be completed within a sprint or less.
- T – Testable; there is a way to validate the completion.

JULY 12

"Give me a lever long enough and a fulcrum on which to place it, and I shall move the world."

- Archimedes

People working are agile is not supposed to work hard. Being agile means that you do just enough to satisfy your customers while adapting to their changing need. It is probably one of the reasons that we often emphasize the importance of focus and prioritization. We want to be effective and efficient.

It is important to note that efficiency, as nice as it sounds is not the goal. One can be efficient in building the wrong thing on time and on budget. It is still the wrong thing to build, thus zero value to one's customers. There it is very important to be effective – to be having the desired effect such as customer satisfaction by building the right thing, on the right time, at right cost.

Doing only what is needed, when it is needed and nothing more is also one of the key concepts in Lean with its relentless effort in the elimination of waste. Speaking of waste, there are 7 wastes according to the Toyota Production System (and 8 in the American version of Lean) they are (remembered as TIM WOODs)

1. Transport – transporting people, tools, inventory or equipment
2. Inventory – finished product waiting to be sold.
3. Motion – unnecessary walking, lifting, reaching, extra clicks.
4. Waiting – people waiting for materials or vice versa.
5. Over Production – producing more than can be sold.
6. Over Processing – doing more than required by customers.
7. Defects – product is not fit for use, need rework.
8. Skills (8th Waste) – waste of human potential.

JULY 13

Every one, well maybe, almost everyone, knows and practices systems thinking. If I want to be able to hike 10 miles, I need to have the right shoes, have the right amount energy (eat) When it is 105 degrees in Austin, TX, I should probably rethink my plan etc., Understanding systems thinking is understanding the complex relationship between a set of obvious, and some not-so-obvious, causes of effects.

In today, often component-driven product development teams, each team may handle different components of a whole product. Each team and component have its own, and sometimes, unique systems or processes. An effort to standardize or optimize the process in one place may end up causing problems in other components.

Phil D. asked us to think of the system as an orchestra. Each musician is his/her own expert. Their contributions are only meaningful when they operate in sync. A bass player deciding to play louder or faster will cause problems. Any player can individually cause the orchestra to cease to be an orchestra and possibly turn into a runaway trainwreck.

The Cobra Problem is an example of the unintended consequences that can occur when attempting to fix a problem without fully considering the system as a whole. The British Colonial in India offered bounty for dead cobras in order to control the cobra population. People ended up breeding cobras to collect the bounties – as a result, the population of cobra increased rather than decreased.

JULY 14

"The electric light did not come from the continuous improvement of candles."

- Oren Harari

This quote is quite controversial. If you look at it from the point of view candle and electric light as let's say, a source of illumination, then electric light can be an evolution of a candle. However, when you look at it as the possible linear progression of a product, it will be very difficult to make the leap from producing candles to producing electric light.

I think that's what Oren Harari tried to demonstrate – that electric light is not a product of **continuous improvement (kaizen)** of candles. Rather, electric light is the product of **radical improvement (kaikaku)** of candles. Japanese management who brought us kaizen (continuous improvement) realized that in certain circumstances, it is not enough to evolve but to take a revolutionary leap and perform radical improvement steps instead.

Jack Welch told the story of the invention of Japan bullet train (when talking about SMART & Stretch Goals). After World War II, Japan embarked in the process of transforming its nation. The economy was growing and every day, thousands of people travel 320 miles between Osaka and Tokyo. In 1955, the trip took around 20 hours. The head of Japan Railway challenged his team to build faster train. Several months later, the team unveiled a "high-speed" train that could travel at 65 miles per hour. The head of Japan Railway said that 65 miles an hour was not going to transform the nation and challenged them to come up with train that could travel up to 120 miles per hour. At first, they said it was impossible. Then they got to work. They had to upgrade everything and a couple years later, the team delivered a 120-mile per -hour train. Cutting the Osaka – Tokyo trip from 20 hours to around 4 hours.

JULY 15

"The most basic way to get someone's attention is to break a pattern."

- Heath Brothers

Paul Rulken pointed out in his TED Talk (if you are interested – search for Paul Rulken TED Talk) that "the purpose of thinking is to stop thinking!"

Neuroscientists will tell you that thinking is very energy-consuming. Based on this information, whoever originated the old saying of a "penny for your thought" probably knew something about it. Although, it probably cost much, much more than a penny. Because thinking is expensive, our brain will try to do it as little as possible. So, when something becomes routine (or if there is a predictable pattern), our brain will stop thinking and relegate the task to autopilot. Paul said that more than 95% of our lives are conducted on autopilot.

So, when we do our activities at work, let's say, a daily stand-up where we mumbled "ah – I did something yesterday, planning to do something else today, no blockers" we are not getting any value. Same thing with Retrospective where people immediately write down "what went well, what didn't go well, what needs improvement." To get people out of the autopilot, break the predictable pattern. Ask different questions, and switch things around. When something different shows up in our brain – we stop the autopilot, pay attention and start thinking again. This is something that Sriram B. has been doing very well.

Note, isn't it also interesting that we use the term "pay attention."

JULY 16

Psychological safety is defined as a shared belief that it is OK to take risk, to express our ideas and concerns, to speak up or question and to admit mistakes without any fear of negative consequences. A team that has a strong sense of psychological safety will become a strong-performing team. A major study conducted by Google concluded that having psychological safety is one of the key ingredients of great team.

The opposite of having psychological safety is the feeling or the need to do everything you can to "cover your ass" (CYA). People that CYA tend to spend most of their time and resources worrying about getting in trouble for coloring outside the line. People tend to spend time only doing what they know, not trying anything new. Innovation becomes stagnant and the team turn into a bunch of zombies only doing what they were told and nothing else.

One of the most insidious impacts of CYA contributed to the Deepwater Horizon disaster in 2010. There was a moment when they had time to prevent the disaster. An engineer standing next to the Emergency Disconnect Switch (EDS) and was prevented from doing so because "He cannot EDS without the OIM's (Offshore Installation Manager's) approval"

How do you foster psychological safety? One of the key components of safety is trust. And one of the key components in building trust is transparency. So, start being transparent. Uncertainties create distrust. Be empathetic, show your fellow team members that you are in this together. Or as Harry Bosch put it "everybody counts, or no one does."

JULY 17

"The IKEA Effect: Cognitive bias in which consumers place a disproportionately high value on products they partially created."
- Michael Norton, Daniel Mochon & Dan Ariely

Have realized that we tend to put more value of the things that we own? If we have an idea and we think that it is a great idea, and then people start talking and even pointing out flaws in the idea, we tend to get defensive about it. Or maybe, sometimes, we are on the other side and can't understand why someone can suddenly turn defensive when we provide, what we think are positive suggestions.

This is known as the IKEA effect, yes, *that* IKEA. Although the term IKEA effect is fairly new, the concept observation of this cognitive bias is not. Aristotle observed a similar phenomenon and said, *"For most things are differently valued by those who have them and by those who wish to get them: what belongs to us, and what we give away, always seems very precious to us."* The phenomenon observed by Aristotle is also known as the Endowment Effect. The Endowment Effect basically pointed out that the very act of owning it (let alone "building" it) is enough for us to put greater value on things.

As we work, we need to keep close attention to our own cognitive biases (and understand others) to allow up to improve the quality of our work, accept feedback more gracefully by seeing the value that it could provide to improve our own instead of hiding in our caves and protecting our own precious ideas or creation. You could turn into Gollum and keep screaming "My precious!"

JULY 18

"People don't pay for values; they pay for perceived value."

- Joe Polish

I'm quite certain that you have heard of, and some maybe have grown tired of hearing, delivering value. What is *value* anyway? Value is one of these things that is very easy to understand yet very difficult to explain. One of the reasons is possibly because, often, value is relative.

The following story has been circulating on the internet; not sure of the original creator.

"A father gave his daughter his old car, one that he has had for many, many years. He told the daughter to bring it to the nearest used car dealer and see how much she could get out of it. The daughter came back and reported the dealer offered her $1,000 for the old car. The father then asked the daughter to bring the car to a pawnshop. The daughter found out that the pawnshop was only willing to give her $200 for it. The father then asked the daughter to bring it to car club. The car club valued the car at more than $100,000 because it was an iconic and much sought-after car."

People value things differently. To maximize your value, you must know your strengths and weaknesses (what are your value propositions). You must find the right conditions (right timing, the right customer segment and the right customer). One way to help understand what your customer needs is by using a Persona when deciding what will be valued.

JULY 19

"The test of a first-rate intelligence is the ability to hold two opposed ideas in the mind at the same time, and still retain the ability to function."

- F. Scott Fitzgerald

Is it possible for someone to have an exact opposite idea to yours and that both you and the person are still correct? It sounds impossible, doesn't it? How could two, clearly opposing ideas be correct at the same time?

We are a product of our upbringing, experiences, culture and biases. We often look at the world through our own specific set of glasses and interpret them. Therefore, it is possible that two opposing ideas could be correct (within certain parameters).

A similar illustration from Buddhist text may explain this better.

There was one a group of blind men who went to see an elephant. The first person touched the elephant's trunk and declared that an elephant is like a thick snake. The second person touched the ear and declared that "You are mistaken. An elephant is like a fan. The third person happened to touch the leg and said that the elephant was like a tree trunk. Another touched the body and declared that it was like a wall. One touched the tusk and said that it was hard and smooth, like a spear and the las person touched the tail and proudly said that "all of you don't know what you are talking about. The elephant is like rope."

So, before you declare someone is wrong just because they have different ideas to yours, try to see the picture that they be right (to a point) after all.

JULY 20

"Any substantial improvement must come from action on the system, the responsibility of management. Wishing and pleading and begging the workers to do better was totally futile."

- W. Edwards Deming

We talked about continuous improvement (kaizen) earlier. Agile teams are very good (or, *supposedly* very good) in continuously improving. It's in their DNA. Continuous improvement is some that can be started by anyone.

We also talked about radical improvement (kaikaku) and it is something that cannot be started by anyone. If one has the idea that could revolutionize an industry, chances are that the person may create a startup and reap the benefit of that radical improvement for him/herself. Meaningful organization improvement must come from the "system" also known as "the management."

One example of a system failure was the space shuttle Challenger disaster in 1986. The Challenger disaster was the result of a combination of factors, including a design flaw in the shuttle's solid-fuel rocket booster and a decision to launch the shuttle despite the known risk of catastrophic failure. The strong data driven culture at NASA at that time prevented the engineer who had concern over the O rings performance in cold weather to prevent the launch because he didn't have all the data he needed to prove that there could be an issue.

W. Edwards Deming strongly believed that the people are already their best and it is the responsibility of the management to provide the right tools and processes to help elevate the people. Punishing, pleading and persuading people to do better, or work harder doesn't work.

JULY 21

"Why, sometimes I've believed as many as six impossible things before breakfast."

- Lewis Carroll

There is an interesting book that I read called "The As If Principle" written by Richard Wiseman. The book talks about a theory created by a Victorian philosopher, William James. The theory states that our feelings don't guide our actions. On the contrary, it was our actions that guide our feelings. Sort of like the statement, "Fake it until you make it." – apparently, according to the principle, you can really make it, by faking it. Often at work, we often see people listening to some ideas, approaches or solutions and many started listing many reasons why that something cannot be done. Starting from "it's impossible" to "it's too expensive to do," to "it's not how we do things here!"

Progress requires the challenging of the status quo. Many things that people thought were impossible are now taken for granted. Some science fiction items have become facts (AI, robots, voice-commands, video calls etc.). Talking about video calls, remember the Agile Manifesto? Principle no. 6 of the manifesto stated that "The most efficient and effective method of conveying information to and within a development team is face-to-face conversation." I would like to point out that when the manifesto was written, the technology for video calling was still in its infancy. People can communicate much better, more effectively and efficiently, remotely. That being said, it still won't replace the camaraderie and non-transactional communications that we get in person. If you talk to Nivi B. and Leo they will tell you the immense importance of communications.

Note. One of the authors of the manifesto clarified that when they said "face-to-face" they would consider video recording as face-to-face communication because you can see the body language.

JULY 22

"Three Principles of Kanban: 1. Start with what you do now; 2. Agree to pursue incremental, evolutionary change; 3. Encourage acts of leadership at all levels."
- David Anderson

The term "Kanban" literally means "signal card." Taiichi Ohno of the Toyota Production System created "Kanban" system to help him control work and inventory so that Toyota, having much smaller demand than the U.S. cars at that time, can build cars only when there is a demand for it. Kanban system was created to signal a pull event from the customer, thus generating production. Although Taiichi Ohno used the term "Kanban" (he didn't invent it either, Kanban is a common word for signboards.) the idea of signaling using card was invented in a U.S. supermarket. At that time, Japan was fascinated by how large U.S. supermarkets manage their inventory.

There are two kinds of Kanban in software development. A kanban board (typically made of columns with different statuses) and Kanban Method as a leaner software development method (created by David A. Anderson)

Kanban (both as a pull system and a method) is not easy, despite what some may have believed. It is highly customized (one can have an unlimited number of columns in kanban, dependent on the flow of work) – it took Taiichi Ohno about ten years to implement his Kanban successfully. As far as the method is concerned, Kanban requires a lot of discipline – there is no guide (unlike Scrum) so to implement Kanban successfully, you really need to know it very well. I consider Kanban as an advanced agile project management tool.

JULY 23

"A fine quotation is a diamond in the hand of a man of wit and a pebble in the hand of a fool."

- Joseph Roux

Beware of buzzwords, including the ones you read in this book. I'm sure that you still remember that our brains are lazy (because thinking is expensive,) so we try to have as many shortcuts, or heuristics – rule of thumbs, as possible. Buzzwords and pithy quotes generally satisfy the criteria. Just because it sounded logical, and someone famous may have said it, it might not always be true.

Consider the popular saying "Absence makes the heart grows fonder – Sextus Aurelius" and the opposite "Out of sight, out of mind – Homer Odyssey." Which one is true? Quote properly, the right circumstances, both are perfectly plausible.

Or this quote that is often attributed to Albert Einstein – "Everyone is a genius. But if you judge a fish by its ability to climb a tree, it will live its whole life believing that it is stupid." It makes sense that Einstein would have said it, he was a genius. Or maybe this quote from Confucius "With great power comes great electricity bills." (OK – I made this last one up!)

So, before we let our mind lazily latch on an idea because it's buzzworthy and pithy, take a moment and do your Google (or Bing) search and if it something is more likely to be true or not.

Note. I am sure that some of the quotes in this book are also misattributed. If you find them, please let me know.

JULY 24

"A good plan, violently executed now, is better than a perfect plan next week."

- *George Patton*

Ansel Adams "Moonrise, Hernandez, New Mexico" is one of the most iconic photographs in history.

Ansel Adam saw an opportunity, he recalled "We were sailing southward along the highway not far from Espanola when I glanced to the left and saw an extraordinary situation – an inevitable black & white photograph! I almost ditched the car and rushed to set up my 8 x 10 camera. I had a clear visualization of the image I wanted, but I could not find my Weston exposure meter! The situation was desperate: the low sun was trailing the edge of clouds in the west, and shadow would soon dim the white crosses." He was a perfectionist and he decided that in this situation, getting is done is better than perfect and he shot the picture without the right meter. He was right. After he took the shot, the moment passed, and the light changed. Moonrise, Hernandez, New Mexico is the story of an iconic image that almost never happened.

I almost drown when my kayak tipped a few years ago. I didn't have life jacket on and the only flotation device was the upside down kayak. I didn't have a lot of time to come up with perfect. I just needed to hang on to the only flotation device I had. I managed to get to safety, one hand holding to the kayak and one hand waddling.

Often time, having an imperfect plan is much better than jumping in without any plan at all, or waiting until you have a perfect plan in the future. It is preferable to act decisively, take the trial-and-error path and refine your process over time than to be paralyzed by waiting for the perfect plan.

JULY 25

"A goal without a plan is just a wish."

- Antoine de Saint-Exupery

Every Sprint, during planning, you are often asked to articulate your Sprint goals. This is because having a goal, a set direction, helps you focus on taking only the steps or path that brings you closer to your desired destination.

This also shows, again, that having a plan to achieve your goal is crucial. Well, maybe not so much as **having** a plan per se but having gone through the process of planning. I believe that having gone through the process of planning is much, much more important than the plan itself. Plans are fallible. We plan, often based on our prediction of the future, and our predictions are often inaccurate. We often plan without having all the perfect information. So, as a result, the planning output a.k.a. "the plan", is often imperfect. And it's OK. That's reason why we have implemented Lean Change Management Process. Something that Princess Renae E. can tell everyone how great and valuable it is in allowing us to have some lofty goals and still be able to change or pivot as we discover new information.

Going through the process of planning forces us to be more deliberate. It forces us to think through what we want to do, how to get there, what should be aware of, what are the potential pitfalls, benefits, etc. Going through this process forces us to consider contingencies, face the facts, gather information and be ready. These are something that should always be front and center in our focus. So even though, our plans may eventually have to change (because it wasn't accurate), our mental models are ready because we have already considered all elements that you could possibly think of and when we react to changes, we react based on something that we have already known.

JULY 26

"A lack of understanding of the theory leaves you unable to differentiate between a necessary aspect of a method and an arbitrary one."

- John Yorke

Clayton Christensen, in his book "The Prosperity Paradox" stated that he was often asked to offer opinions on specific business challenges in the domains that he has no special knowledge of. He was able to provide insight because he has a toolbox of theories that teach him not what to think, rather how to think about a problem. He concluded that understanding theory helps us to understand the underlying mechanism of how things work. Good theory helps us focus on the practical question of what causes what - and why.

To further illustrate the point, he gave an example of human's early attempts to fly. For thousands of years, we have dreamt taking to the skies. The quest has led from kite flying in ancient China to hydrogen-powered hot-air balloons in 18th-century France. Many, including Leonardo DaVinci, observed a strong correlation between being able to fly and having feathers and wings. Some strapped themselves with feathers and wings, jumped from cathedrals and flapped hard only to end up flat on the grounds (pun intended). It wasn't until Daniel Bernoulli, introduced a concept of fluid dynamic, which stated that pressure decreases when the flow speed increases (later known as the Bernoulli's principle) that we evolved our understanding from correlation (feathers and wings) to causation (weight, lift, drag and thrust). It was the understanding that eventually enabled the Wright brothers to make the first controlled, sustained flight from Kitty Hawk, North Carolina.

Having a theory allows one to fully understand how or why something happened, thus one can apply the same theory to solve different problems not just blindly trying to apply the same solution to every problem.

JULY 27

"A lean production system can seem almost supernatural to an inexperienced observer. People, processes, and technology magically seem to appear at the right time, do exactly what is needed, and no more."

- James P. Womack and Daniel T. Jones

The term "lean" was first coined by John Krafcik in his 1998 article "Triumph of the Lean Production System" contrasting the Toyota Production System (TPS) to the more "bloated/fat" production practiced by the US car manufacturers.

Everything that we do, can be made leaner because, as Womack and Jones defined it "lean is a way to do more and more with less and less – less human effort, less equipment, less time and less space – while coming closer and closer to providing customers exactly what they want."

They define the following five principles of lean:

1. Define Value – you need to know what your customers value.
2. Map the Value Stream – map all the steps/activities it takes for you to deliver the value to your customer. Remove any waste in the steps.
3. Create Flow – ensure a smooth flow of the value to customers!
4. Establish Pull – allow the customer to signal you when they want the value delivered. (Note, it took Taiichi Ohno 10 years to perfect this flow by using Kanban.)
5. Pursue Perfection – continuously improve the process (kaizen).

Kristi D. is one of the few people whom I have worked with that embodies the spirit of lean. She is continuously improving and getting closer to closer to providing customers exactly what they want.

JULY 28

"A team is not a group of people who work together. A team is people who trust each other."

- Simon Sinek

If you see ten people waiting in line to watch a basketball game, would you call them a team? How about if you see four golfers playing in a foursome for individual scores? You wouldn't call them a "team" because they are not. Just doing things together doesn't make them a team. As Simon Sinek pointed out one of (if not "the") key requirements for team building is trust. So, how do you build trust? Now, that's a toughie. Trust is not something that can be given. It is something that must be earned. Because it must be earned, it is not something that someone else has to do. It's you. Whether you can earn someone's trust or not is beyond your control. You must behave in ways to send a signal that you are worthy of trust.

The subject on how to build trust can fill a library, but since all (well, almost all) of you are familiar with the Scrum framework, I would like to introduce "the 5 values of Scrum." They are:

1. Focus – that the team focus on delivering highest value.
2. Respect – team respect each other and **all** stakeholders.
3. Openness – team are honest when they need help.
4. Courage – team must feel safe enough to say so, ask for help or to try new things.
5. Commitment – team are committed to each other first, they follow through on what they say they would.

If you need a hack on how to get people to start trusting you, ask for help. People like someone who ask them for favor (this is known as The Benjamin Franklin Effect. Go Google it. It's interesting.)

JULY 29

"Adding manpower to a late software project makes it later."

- Fred Brooks

Martin L. reminded me of this quote. It is also known as the "Brooks' Law." It was first coined in the book "The Mythical Man-Month: Essays on Software Engineering." The central theme of the book is that "adding manpower to a software project that is behind schedule delays it even longer."

Fred Brooks explained that this happened because:
1. It takes some time before the new "manpower" can get up speed and start contributing. In the meantime, he/she is taking cycle from existing developers by asking questions.
2. Communications overhead increases. You can use the Communication Channel formula of $N * (N-1) / 2$ to calculate the possible exponential growth of the number of comm channels. A team of 6 will have 15 channels and a team of 7 will have 21 channels. Adding one person will result in an additional 40% more channels.
3. People may get in the way of each other in some circumstances. Fred popularized the analogy that while it takes one woman nine months to make one baby, "nine women can't make a baby in one month."

That being said, I have seen that the law doesn't always prevail (Fred recognized that too – he called this law an oversimplification.) If the person added is familiar with the work, he/she can really hit the ground running with almost no set-up time. The key here is to not expect a totally new resource to be able to rescue a late project. It is better to take a different approach, such as by focusing only the most important items (the must haves) or to start getting the new resource early in the project.

JULY 30

"Adopting agile can feel worse before it feels better. Problems and tensions often become more visible, which can be uncomfortable for some teams. But when tensions are more visible, you have a better opportunity to solve them."

- Jordan Husney

Many people mistakenly believe that adopting agile framework (especially the famous frameworks – just in case you are wondering, Scrum is the most famous agile framework, being used by more than 87% of organizations) is going to solve all their problems. They are, how should I say nicely, well – ***mistaken.***

This is despite the claim by Jeff Sutherland, a co-creator of Scrum, in his book "Scrum: The Art of Doing Twice the Work in Half the Time." He mentioned that Scrum doesn't solve your problems. Scrum just show you how screwed you are. The idea is that once you have seen the headlight of on oncoming train, you will decide that you need to do something about it.

And it is not just Scrum. Same principle applies to all software development framework and methodology. Fred Brooks wrote a paper on software engineering with the title "No Silver Bullet" where he argued that ""there is no single development, in either technology or management technique, which by itself promises even one order of magnitude [tenfold] improvement within a decade in productivity, in reliability, in simplicity."

The other creator of Scrum – Ken Schwaber painted another vivid picture that "Scrum is like your mother-in-law; it points out all your faults." It is up to you, to fix the problems. Iteratively, of course!

JULY 31

"All animals are equal, but some are more equal than others."

- George Orwell

Someone told me that this quote from the Animal Farm by George Orwell is not the best quote to talk about prioritization, maybe a little bit too Orwellian, they say.

Well, it's here, in this book. Stubbornness aside, I really think that there is no better saying to illustrate the often-subjective nature of prioritization. Matthew C. can probably write a book about the complexity involved in good prioritization. There are a lot of great prioritization matrix out there, is many cases, someone's priority may be higher than yours, and that is the way. There are some techniques you can adopt, like: (not in any order of importance)

a) R.I.C.E – Reach, Impact, Confidence & Effort. The formula is RICE = (Reach * Impact * Confidence) / Effort

b) M.o.S.C.o.W – for Must Have, Should Have, Could Have and Won't Have.

c) Impact vs., Effort Matrix

d) Value vs. Complexity / Effort matrix

e) Weighted Shortest Job First (WSJF) – consist of User Business Value, Time Criticality and Risk Reduction / Opportunity Enablement divided by Job Size. The sum of User Business Value, Time Criticality and Risk Reduction / Opportunity is known is the Cost of Delay.

f) Cost of Delay Divided by Duration (CD3) technique. As the name suggest – this method only consider Cost over Time. (If this looks like WSJF, it is because WSJF was built upon CD3 technique created by Don Reinertsen.

g) Kano Model - Dissatisfier, Basic and Exciter

h) $100 Test or Monopoly Money. And more.

AUGUST

AUGUST 1

"An error doesn't become a mistake until you refuse to correct it."

- O.A. Battista

We were shooting the breeze the other day and someone asked if the color orange comes before the fruit or the fruit comes before the color. I know, from time to time, we like to solve the world's problem. After solving the world's problem, we talked about which comes first, chicken or egg, and eventually moved on the unsolvable age-old questions of "why does the chicken cross the road?"

We also talked about the tolerance for errors. It is a fact of life that everyone, I mean **everyone**, makes mistakes. (If you believe that you have never made any mistakes in your life, let's talk. I have a beachfront property in Arizona that I want to sell!). Making a mistake (or error) is not a bad thing. It may be signs that we are trying something new. Building or doing something new, is very much in line with the idea of being agile. One of the most important things we do when we make mistakes is to learn from it and to adapt.

Not all mistakes are bad. Alexander Fleming, accidentally discovered lifesaving medicine because he made a mistake. He left his bacteria culture out overnight and when he returned the next day, he found some mold growing on his culture. That mold was called Penicillium notatum or penicillin.

This is one of the reasons why conducting retrospective is very important. It doesn't really matter if you are using Scrum or Kanban – one should always, always learn from the past and strive to become better. Remember that good judgment comes from experience, and experience comes from bad judgment. Iterate, always iterate.

AUGUST 2

The morning of January 13, 2018 was a warm sunny day in Honolulu, Hawaii. Tourists were enjoying a nice Saturday morning and suddenly at 8:07 a.m. local time, people started receiving emergency alert on their phones as well as television broadcast. The message read, in all caps "BALLISTIC MISSILE THREAT INBOUND TO HAWAII. SEEK IMMEDIATE SHELTER. THIS IS NOT A DRILL." After everybody panicked and it wasn't until 8:20 a.m. – a very long 13 minutes, an official message refuting the alert was sent out. After an internal investigation, the person who made that mistake was fired 13 days later. (I am sure all this recurring number 13 is just a pure coincidence. I really am. Really.)

That was a bad judgment and the person learned from it. I have always joked about the fact that he/she (the person's gender was never revealed) should be allowed to keep the job. I can guarantee that the person will never, ever make the same mistake again. But of course, what if there was a real emergency and the person, being gun-shy now, hesitated. The repercussion can be bad.

Vernon Law said that "experience is a bad teacher because she gives the test first, the lesson afterward." Also, realistically, we don't have time to experience everything. Our goal is, whenever possible, to live vicariously through the experience of others. If we must experience something ourselves, the best way to do it is to try to create a controlled environment. Test our product with small audience to minimize the impact. Practice solving hairy problems in test or controlled environments. Netflix popularized the practice of "chaos monkey" to allow their team to experience disaster, within a controlled environment. So that when the disaster actually happened, the team would have "experienced" it.

40

AUGUST 3

"Any   sufficiently   advanced   technology   is indistinguishable from magic."

- Arthur C. Clarke

Good developers are like magician. The things that they can achieve just by mostly using the if-then loop. Heck, to take it even more magical, it was all done in binary – just ones and zeros strung together. And when all these ones and zeros and if-then works, they are magical. And when they don't, it can be frustrating. Larry Niven observed "That's the thing about people who think they hate computers. What they really hate is lousy programmers."

Good software development is now (well, has been for quite a while) a team sport. Gone are the days when a lone, sleep-deprived, developer hacking away in a basement, all night to release some new software. And it is a good thing. Many studies have proven that things that are built by diverse people (diverse as in skills, background, experiences – and not just gender and race) are much better than a single individual.

So, teamwork and teams create magic. Teamwork is the ultimate competitive advantage. Unfortunately, some teams are dysfunctional. The absence of trust is the key to all dysfunctions. Patrick Lencioni codified the Five Dysfunctions of a Team in a book with that same name. They are:

1. The Absence of Trust
2. Fear of Conflict
3. Lack of Commitment
4. Avoidance of Accountability
5. Inattention to Results

So, remember, build trust, build team, make magic!

AUGUST 4

"All we are doing is looking at the timeline, from the moment the customer gives us an order to the point when we collect the cash. And we are reducing the timeline by reducing the non-value adding wastes."

- Taiichi Ohno

We talked about mapping the value stream earlier. What Taiichi Ohno described in the quote is the definition of mapping the value stream. The purpose of mapping the value stream is not to have a value stream. The purpose is to understand the flow of value back to the customer starting from the moment the value was requested (an order is given) and once understood, to start reducing the timeline by reducing the non-value adding wastes.

Imagine the time we went to our neighborhood taco stand. We were shown a place to sit down, given a menu, left alone to think and try to solve world hunger problem, decided which taco we want, the attendant returned, took the order on a pad, walked back to the kitchen, hollered two fish tacos, slapped the order note on a magnetic hanging thingy, cook grab the note, cook started making our taco, hollered order no. 42 is ready, attendant walked back to the kitchen, grabbed the taco, walked to us, gave us the taco, said "enjoy the taco, is there anything else you need?" We wolfed the taco down in 2 minutes flat, walk up to the cashier, pay and leave.

The only value for us was when we wolfed down the tacos. The attendant walking back and forth, asking us to enjoy the taco, writing down orders may be non-value-added activities. Some non-value-added activities needs to be eliminated but some are necessary. The key is to identify those activities and figure out a way to either remove them, reduce them or to optimize them, with the end goal of the exchange of cash for value.

AUGUST 5

"You can't hit a target you cannot see, and you cannot see a target you do not have."

- Zig Ziglar

There are a lot of goals or objective in our line of work. Our company has Objectives and Key Results (OKR), every quarter during the quarterly planning cycle, you are asked to have quarterly goals, every two weeks, during your Sprint Planning, you must articulate your team's Sprint Goal.

Having a goal is important because it provides you with direction and focus. It forces you to channel your efforts towards something meaningful. Goals also provide us with a forward momentum, help boost a sense of achievement.

Having a goal is also a great motivator. Simon Sinek in his book "Drive: The Surprising Truth About What Really Motivate Us" identified three factors that motivate people.

1. Purpose – in this case, having a goal gives us clarity to understand our work.
2. Autonomy – being trusted to solve our own problems.
3. Mastery – having the opportunity to be very good at what we are doing.

What happens if you don't bother to have a goal? Well, Yogi Berra – the master of stating the obvious stated, "If you don't know where you're going, you might not get there."

AUGUST 6

"Civilization advances by extending the number of important operations which we can perform without thinking about them."

- Alfred North Whitehead

Remember the discussion about the purpose of thinking is to stop thinking? That because thinking is "expensive" our brain tries to do it as little as possible. Whenever our brain detects a pattern, it will create a mental model and automate the function.

Advancement of technology often has its detractors. In the early 19th century, there was a group of artisans and craftsmen who opposed the use of machines in manufacturing. They feared that these machines will jeopardize their job and livelihood. They attacked factories and destroyed weaving machines. These groups called themselves the Luddites, after 'King Ludd" – a mythical character who lived in Sherwood Forest. They failed and today the term Luddite is used to refer to someone who is resistant to or afraid of new technology.

There are always people who are afraid of progress. When the internet was invented (by Al Gore, said Al Gore, wink – wink) many said that would be the end of the libraries. Didn't happen. One of the most current examples is chatgpt, some teachers are afraid that students no longer need to learn, write papers, etc., I would say, "Check it out! Learn what this technology could do for you, and you could use it to augment your capabilities. One of Toyota core practices is called Jidoka or Autonomation – automation with human intelligence. Do you remember the movie "Johnny Mnemonic"? – If I can have a cybernetic implant to augment my capacity for memory, I will sign up in a hot minute.

On a side note, anyone working on QA or CI/CD should strive to be more like our brain. Whenever there is a pattern, automate the function.

AUGUST 7

*"Begin at the beginning," the King said, very gravely,
"and go on till you come to the end: then stop."*

- Lewis Carroll

With all due respect to the king in the 'Alice in the Wonderland" by Lewis Carroll, *where is the beginning?* - in Alice's case, was the beginning in the morning when she woke up, or was it when she decided to follow the white rabbit? or some could argue it was the time she was born (that's *the* beginning, right?) Some would argue maybe the time her parents met or maybe, just maybe the big bang *is* the beginning.

You can see how thinking like this can be paralyzing. Some people encounter a similar problem working on projects. At least in the predictive project management methodology the answer can be quite clear – the beginning of the project is when the project charter is created or signed. There is often a lack of absolute beginning in iterative project management. (Some instituted a Sprint 0 where the team can prep their backlog.) Regardless of where you might get involved in the project, getting started is key. Jose L. may not have gotten involved in his Artemis project from the very beginning, but as soon as he got involved, he took his first step and ran with it. The great results, speak for itself.

So, instead of being paralyzed by this potential arbitrary beginning, why don't you just begin. Just start. Starting here and now, is better than waiting for the perfect tomorrow. It is better than lamenting the could haves, should haves and would haves. Start where you are. Take the first step. Evaluate your direction and improve as you go. Lao Tzu advised that "A journey of a thousand *li* begins with the first step." A very wise advice from a very wise man.

AUGUST 8

"Don't let life discourage you; everyone who got where he is had to begin where he was."

- Richard L. Evans

Well, maybe not *everyone*. You could be born into the Rockefeller dynasty or get married to Bill Gates daughter. *Everyone else*, had to begin where they were.

Speaking about starting where we are, let's talk more about Kanban as a method (not kanban as the board). I mentioned the three principles of Kanban, and some would disagree and say that – no there are four principles of kanban, no – five, wait six. It seems like a it is a moving target. The three principles of Kanban that we talked about earlier were created by David Anderson – the pioneer of Kanban Method.

They are confusing because Mr. Anderson [get it? Mr. Anderson?] categorized the principles into two.

a) Change Management Principles
   1. Start with what you do now.
   2. Agree to pursue improvement through evolutionary change.
   3. Encourage acts of leadership at all levels.

b) Service Oriented Principles
   1. Understand and focus on customer needs and expectations.
   2. Manage the work; let people self-organize around it.
   3. Regularly review the network of services and its policies in order to improve outcomes.

Now you know why sometimes it's three and sometimes it's six.

AUGUST 9

"Customer with a purpose won't pay attention to what we want until we satisfy what they want first."

- Paco Underhill

I think I would have made Yogi Berra proud when I say, "product development is hard." Sometimes, people make the mistakes of thinking that they know exactly what the customers need. Now, they may not always be wrong. Steve Jobs knew that we all need iPads before we even knew that we wanted them. Unfortunately, there are not a lot of Steve Jobs to go around. Or Jeff Bezos for that matter.

The second-best thing we could do then is to understand our customers – that our customers will only engage with us, will give us their time (and money) *after* we have met their needs first. It is paramount that we understand customer's pain points and preferences so that we build solutions that work for them. The effort of understanding is the customer is made harder by the fact that what the customer tells us they want, may not be what they really want. This is one of the reasons why Paco Underhill – author of "Why We Buy: The Science of Shopping" sent "spies" to follow shoppers around in supermarkets so that he can observe what people actually do instead of hearing what people say they do. This is known as an ethnographic research, where we observe our customers going through their daily routines. He didn't rely on video recordings because they don't capture all the nuances. Of course, if you have been to the latest Amazon GO stores, you will know that this is no longer true. If you pick your nose inside an Amazon GO store, Jeff Bezos will know it. So, watch out!

Anyway, with everything that we do and build, start from the customer and work backwards. They are, after all, our raison d'etre. Our reason for being.

AUGUST 10

"Coming together is a beginning, staying together is progress, and working together is success."

- Henry Ford

You are familiar with the stages of team development – also known as Tuckman's Stages of Group Development. This was proposed by Bruce Tuckman. Do you know that his middle name is Wayne. Wouldn't it be so cool if this was called Bruce Wayne Stages of Group Development?

Tuckman proposed that there are five stages of group development.
1. Forming – the team is formed. Everyone plays nice and avoid conflict because they want to be accepted. They learn where they fit in the system – I would call this the honeymoon period.
2. Storming – once people know their place, some will start pushing the boundaries and conflicts occur. Differences are accentuated. This is a tough time – a make or break moment.
3. Norming – if the team made it past the previous stage, they start to see the commonalities instead of differences. They agree on the common goals. They are starting to develop trust and asking people for help. They started collaborating. This is where most teams are.
4. Performing – the team is stable; the goals are clear. They have developed a working rhythm. They have shared knowledge, face challenges together. It's almost to the point where they utter half sentences, and the other team member will know exactly what needs to be done. This is the holy grail of team development.
5. Adjourning – this stage was added a dozen years later, where the project is done, and the team is splitting. This is why we try to build long lasting team, so they stay in stage 4 and continually grow together instead of moving to stage 5. Keep in mind that when new person is added, the stages start again from Forming.

AUGUST 11

"Don't move information to authority, move authority to the information."

- L. David Marquet

Once in a while, you may encounter Dilbert-esque decision made by some people in authority and you wonder how did someone in that level of authority miss the mark by that much.

Someone will inevitably point out that there is nothing wrong withit. They even have a name for it. It is called the "Peter's Principle." It states that a person who is competent at their job will earn a promotion to a position that requires different skills. If the promoted person lacks the skills required for the new role, they will be incompetent at the new level, and will not be promoted again. That sounds like a mouthful – I read a simpler version somewhere that says that one is often promoted until they reached their level of incompetence and stays there.

Being the butt of a joke notwithstanding, this problem is real. It is called the Ivory Tower Syndrome. This could happen because leaders, far removed from employees who are in the trenches, are out of touch with reality. Yet they are expected to make high impact decisions. This happened because some still believe that only people with authority must know what they are doing because they are VIP (very important people.)

By the way, just in case you are curious, there is an inverse to the Peter's Principle – and it is called the Dilbert Principle. It states that companies tend to promote their least-competent employees to management roles where they are least likely to interfere with production.

AUGUST 12

"Engineers like to build products using the coolest new technology. Sales wants to build products that will make them a lot of money. But the product manager's sole focus and responsibility is to build the right products for their customers. That's the job."

- Tony Fadell

We talked about how a product development is hard. It really takes a village and then some, to build great products. In this great collaboration, one role stands out more than any other role. The Product Manager.

A Product Manager is often described as someone who sits in the intersection between Business, User Experience (UX) and Technology. Business wants to make money; technology always wants to use the newest and coolest techno-wizardry and User wants great experience. Product Management has the sole responsibility to fulfill all these.

According to Marty Cagan in his book "Inspired: How to Create Tech Products that Customers Love" he identified four key responsibilities of a strong product manager.

1. Deep knowledge of the customer – know their issues, pains, desires, how they think.
2. Deep knowledge of the data – spend time looking at product analytics, looking at results of A/B tests.
3. Deep knowledge of your business - your various stakeholders are and the constraints they operate under.
4. Deep knowledge of your market and industry – including your competitors. Know key trends in technology, customer behaviors and expectations, following the relevant industry analysts.

AUGUST 13

"Every now and then, a man's mind is stretched by a new idea or sensation, and never shrinks to its former dimensions."

- Oliver Wendell Holmes, Sr.

You are familiar with the expression that a chain is only as strong as the weakest link. Same principle can be applied to teamwork. A team is only as strong as the weakest team member.

Of course, you are not the weakest link. You have experience, right? I hope you are not easily deceived by this version of you. In the right context, everyone was once, the weakest link – really everyone – no exception, not even the descendant of the Rockefeller family or the Bill Gates' daughter. In all the cases, someone spent time to help you become a stronger and stronger link.

One of the key practices in Extreme Programming is pair programming. Pair programming is a great way to help your team members to become better and surprisingly, you will find out that it also makes you better. It turns out that the act of teaching or showing someone how to do something helps reinforce what you already know, reevaluate your knowledge and allows you to see from other's point of view. So, when you do pair programming, everyone gets better. Pair programming is like a way that you can pay it forward for the people who built you up.

If you are in the camp that says people need to pull their own weights or they don't belong, I want to reassure you that this is not just some Pollyanna BS. Putting it differently, this could be some of the most self-serving acts that you do. By ensuring and helping that your team member has the right skillset to do their job well, you are ensuring that your team will do well. Helping your teammates to be better is one of the best ways to ensure your own success.

AUGUST 14

"And those who were seen dancing were thought to be insane by those who could not hear the music."

- Friedrich Nietzsche

Have you ever tried to explain something so obvious to your stakeholders or coworkers and couldn't really believe yourself that "they" could have failed to see or understand the obvious?

For example, you often heard the phrase "delivering value" or "win on impact." and from time to time, especially in the middle of the night and you can't bring yourself to sleep, you wonder "what does that even mean?" For the people who use those phrases, they are self-explanatory. We must deliver value to our customers. Right?

People who know their domain very well have years of experiences and the phrase summarizes their wealth of knowledge. But for people who don't have the same experience – it may be just some meaningless jargon. This is called the curse of knowledge. This curse was demonstrated well with a game called the "tapping game" – you use your fingers and tap the song that you know well and have someone try to guess the song. When you rate your own performance, you may rate yourself highly, but the reality is quite crushing. Study showed tappers predicted that 50% of the time, the guessers can guess the right song, and in reality, the success ratio was only 2.5%.

Extreme Programming (XP) uses metaphor to try to explain concept to stakeholders. XP proposed to guide the development team using simple shared story on how the whole system works. In regards of milestone and roadmap – one could say "imagine driving from New Jersey boardwalk to the Santa Monica pier in California. You need to know where you are spending the night (your milestones) and you need to have an overall picture on how and when you get there (your roadmap).

52

AUGUST 15

There was a story about Pablo Picasso. He was sketching in a public park in Paris, when a woman noticed him and asked if he could sketch a portrait of her. Picasso studied the woman and using a single pencil stroke, he sketched her perfectly. She was very impressed at the result asked how much she would need to pay him. Picasso said, "Five thousand Francs!" She was taken aback and said "but, but it only took you a couple second to do it!" Picasso responded "Madame, it took me my entire life to learn how to do it." *(Although Picasso had been known to work in a public park, the detail of the story including the payment may be apocryphal.)*

The story illustrates a very important reason as to why we build software in short iterations. It is not that software cannot be built without working in iterations. Before agile movement, Bell Labs had been building and releasing software using the, so called, Big Bang Release. Where the developers take the complete requirements up front, go away for a year or two, then emerge with a big "ta da!" – on time, in scope and on budget (PMI – Project Management Institute would be proud) except to find out that the customer no longer wants/needs it. The market has moved on.

Agile movement proposed an iterative process with small, and frequent releases, something that Amit A. evangelize every chance he has. Changing and adapting to the latest feedback to keep pace with customer want and need. Agile process enables software development to keep pace and evolve in tandem with the customer's need. This is also one of the reasons that agile do not require perfect requirements up front, because we understand that they will change. We only need requirements to get us through the next few iterations until we need to adapt.

AUGUST 16

"Half-Done Is Not Done. A half-built car simply ties up resources that could be used to create value or save money. Anything that's 'in process' costs money and energy without delivering anything."

- Jeff Sutherland

What does "done" mean to your team? is code complete, done? How about that it already passed QA and waiting to be released? In Jeff Sutherland's point, done is simple. Something is done when it's generating value by being used by the intended customer (I am summarizing here because I am sure he didn't say it like this.)

Suppose your spouse gave you a honey-do list. The dog is hungry, and you are out of dog food, and you need to go buy dog food at your neighborhood Costco. The fallen leaf is making our yard messy, so you need to take care of the problem and finally, because today is laundry Wednesday, you need to do the laundry too. And off your spouse go does whatever spouses usually do after giving the honey-do list..

You hop on your Tesla Model X, got to Costco, grab the dog food, in and out in 10 minutes flat. You are so proud of yourself. Task 1, done. As soon as you put the Tesla back in the garage, you take out the rake, after just 15 minutes, all the leaves are nicely pile up on a corner. Task 2, done. You go inside the house, start the laundry. Laundry done. Have plenty of time to grab a cold one and enjoy the 5th season of the Marvelous Mrs. Maisel in Amazon Prime.

Your spouse came home a couple hours later. Notices that the yard is still messy (apparently as you were enjoying your show, a strong gust of wind redistributed your leaf pile. And that the dog is still hungry and asked about the food. You said, "it's done. It's in the trunk!" – laundry is done but hasn't been put in the dryer yet. So, are they done, done?

AUGUST 17

"Humphrey Law: The user will never know what they want until after the system is in production (maybe not even then.)."

- *Read Somewhere*

I read about the Humphrey's law from Jeff Sutherland's book "Scrum: The Art of Doing Twice the Work in Half the Time" however I am having hard time tracking down the origin. So, will just have to trust Jeff on this.

One of the reasons agile software development works is that because often time, in the beginning, we don't really know for sure what the end-product would be. We may have a pretty good idea about what we think it is, however, the reality may be different. The same principle applies to our stakeholders or even our users.

Using iterative product development allows us to build just enough to validate our hypotheses of the expected result and if it is validated, then we added more to the increment. If not, then we remove the ones that didn't prove the hypotheses and try another solution, one iteration at a time. Sometimes, out stakeholders don't know what they really want. In order to tease out what they really, really want, we can perform an A/B testing. A/B testing is also known as split testing, where we show two or more versions of a variable to different segments of customers at the same time to determine which have better impact and drive business result. We can then tweak the result to keep improving the results. Keep in mind that when we tweak something, we only tweak one thing at a time. Tweaking more than one variable at a time may cause you to potentially misattribute the cause of effect that you are looking for.

AUGUST 18

"I know who I WAS when I got up this morning, but I think I must have been changed several times since then."

- Lewis Carroll

Change is inevitable, growth is optional. Every day we wake up we are being changed. We are encountering changes as well as serving as change agents.

Philosophically speaking aside, change is also an important part of all projects. If you are working on a project that take several months to complete, chances are, there will be changes to the project. Some may mistakenly believe that if there are too many changes to the plan, it was simply because of the failure during planning and next time, we shall plan harder. The reality is that it is not about planning harder.

None of us can predict the future. The person who can predict the future will be the richest person on earth. What we do during project planning is that we take the cone of uncertainty into account. The cone of uncertainty is a concept used in project management to represent the range of possible outcomes for a project. The base of the cone represents our initial assumptions while the tip of the cone represents the possible future outcomes. The best example of the cone of uncertainty in action is the hurricane landfall forecast. The projected path of the hurricane looks almost exactly like the cone of uncertainty. We have a pretty good idea where the project should be headed, but we can't know for sure. So, when the information presents itself and it forces a change, we should do it gladly. We have just learned something valuable about the project, so change, for the lack of a better word, is good!

AUGUST 19

"If you don't collect any metrics, you're flying blind. If you collect and focus on too many, they may be obstructing your field of view."

- Scott M. Graffius

Frederick Winslow Taylor pioneered the scientific management in the 19th century. He was obsessed in collecting metrics in order to find the most efficient way to complete a task. He observed line workers, noted how skilled workers performed their task and engineered ways to optimize each task.

Taylorism manages people by breaking down their job into small, predictable tasks and then optimize those tasks to improve efficiency and reduce waste. Doesn't this sound familiar? Aren't you being asked to break an Epic/Feature down to a set of User Stories? Don't you also often have to break those User Stories down into a set of Tasks? Is agile Taylorism being disguised?

No. The difference is, in Taylorism, the management tells you how long it should take for you to complete your tasks. The management tells you how to do everything. You are just an automaton. Agile recognizes that people are not automaton. People have purpose, people need a sense of mastery and autonomy. Agile trusts people to be creative and inventive. Agile gives people autonomy by using User Stories. A User story represents an intent, the "what". It doesn't dictate "how" one should go about achieving the intent. Agile focuses on maximizing value and customer satisfaction. Taylorism focuses on compliance. In agile, you collect metric so that you, yourself, can evaluate your own performance and decide what you would to improve. By the way, using metric to adjust to plan is something that Shreena R. excelled at.

AUGUST 20

"If you seek to plot out all your moves before you make them—if you put your faith in slow, deliberative planning in the hopes it will spare you failure down the line—well, you're deluding yourself. For one thing, it's easier to plan derivative work—things that copy or repeat something already out there. So, if your primary goal is to have a fully worked out, set-in-stone plan, you are only upping your chances of being unoriginal."

- Ed Catmull

Once upon a time, there were Extreme Programming and Scrum. They had a conference and agile was born (OK, I am taking a lot of liberties and simplifying this, a whole lot!)

Around that time, the idea of lean for software development had also been germinating. Even though the thought leaders from lean were not able to attend the meeting at Snowbird, UT in 2001, Lean Software Development was considered as one of several Agile approaches to software development. Mary & Tom Poppendieck, author of "The Lean Software Development: An Agile Toolkit" published in 2003 solidify lean as an agile approach. *Lean principles were used to explain why Agile methods were better. Lean explained that Agile methods contained little "waste" and hence produced a better economic outcome. Lean principles were used as a "permission giver" to adopt Agile methods.* However, some agile thought leaders argue that the relentless elimination of waste may work against the innovative nature of agility. Lean pursues the elimination of variation (through elimination of wastes) and when everything is optimized to a T, there will be no room for innovation. This argument forgot to take into the account of the relentless empowerment to employee to innovate in order to keep reducing the waste. Once we start looking, there are so many things that we could optimize and improve, and we won't be too lean too quickly and run out of innovations.

AUGUST 21

"If you want to build a ship, don't summon people to buy wood, prepare tools, distribute jobs, and organize the work; teach people the yearning for the wide, boundless ocean."

- Antoine de Saint Exupery

While Taylorism treats an employee as a cog in the wheel, agile treats people as unique individuals. Sometimes, those unique individuals may need to be motivated.

Recall that we mentioned a book titled "Drive: The Surprising Truth About What Really Motivates Us" by Daniel H. Pink. The book talked about studies in human motivation conducted by M.I.T and other universities. The study found that we are not "just" motivated by more money. It found that for work that consists of basic mechanical skills, monetary incentives work. However, if the task involves the use of cognitive skills, decision-making, creativity, or higher-order thinking, higher pay resulted in lower performance.

New York state have more than 1,600 fire departments, 93% of them are made of volunteers. Studies found that those volunteers saved more than $4.5 billions of NY taxpayers. Firefighting is one of the most dangerous jobs and many are doing it for very little to money at all.

According to the book, knowledge workers (that means us), are motivated beyond money. They are motivated by purpose, autonomy and the pursuit of mastery. This doesn't mean that we can pay them peanuts (and give them a lot of purpose, autonomy and the pursuit of mastery.). We still need to pay them enough so that they no longer need to worry about having enough money. People who are not paid adequately, knowledge workers or not, will not be motivated. Daniel Pink suggested that we should pay people enough to take the issue of money off the table.

AUGUST 22

"If you want to have good ideas, you must have many ideas. Most of them will be wrong, and what you have to learn is which ones to throw away."

- Linus Pauling

Steve Jobs said that "People think focus means saying yes to the thing you've got to focus on. But that's not what it means at all. It means saying no to the hundred other good ideas that there are. You have to pick carefully. I'm actually as proud of the things we haven't done as the things I have done. Innovation is saying 'no' to 1,000 things."

I seldom see a product development team that has nothing to do. It is often the opposite, they have too much to do. The task at hands is to weed out the merely good ideas to get to the great ideas. The idea is that the more ideas you have, the more likely you are to come up with a great one. However, not all the ideas you come up with will be good, and it's important to have a process in place to filter out the bad ideas and find the good ones. You can test the ideas against real-world data, customer feedback, and other indicators of whether it's a good idea or not. In agile, you are familiar with the importance of building a Proof of Concept (POC) before spending too much time and effort to build the actual product that people may not want or need. One can even use a Wizard of Oz Prototyping in order to avoid building functional product. Try to experiment by expending the least effort possible.

It's important to understand that to come up with great ideas, you need to have the courage to throw away some of the good ideas and not be afraid to pivot or change direction if it's clear that the idea is not working out. That being said, Anthony Ulwick, with his "Jobs To Be Done" theory pointed out that this "brute-force" innovation doesn't work. Having many ideas doesn't guarantee that you will have the right ideas.

AUGUST 23

"Improving workflow, the way value is created, is a continual source of advantage for the firms that do it. They gain speed, quality, efficiency, and in many cases simplicity. Yet it's routinely overlooked in favor of cosmetic changes to structure that rarely change how work gets done."

- Aaron Dignan

A workflow is described as a sequence of activities through a predetermined path from start to finish.

We are familiar with many workflows. Service Now tickets have a specific workflow once a ticket is opened. Jira tickets have customizable workflows and some prescribed workflow. If you need your Jira customized, Keith V. can do in an instance. You should see the things he could do in Jira.

It is said that if you can't describe your work in a logical workflow, you haven't really understood your tasks. Designing a workflow is very important. Having the right workflow allows predictable value creation as well as identifiable steps that can be improved. David Marquet, author of "Leadership is Language" said that it is important to get the sequence right. We must "close the hatch" first before we can "submerge the submarine" – getting the workflow flip could be disastrous.

We can identify the workflow and then work on optimizing each step. This process is called Value Stream Mapping. Done correctly, Value Stream Mapping can help teams work together more effectively by clearly identifying the dependencies in each step, the handoff and the execution. Once identified, we can work on making them more efficient.

AUGUST 24

"Individual commitment to a group effort: That is what makes a teamwork, a company work, a society work, a civilization work."

- Vince Lombardi

We touched on the 5 values of Scrum earlier and I listed it as Focus, Respect, Openness, Courage and Commitment. The reason why I listed them that way is that because the first letters form a mnemonic of FROCC, and I remember as FROG.

When Jeff Sutherland and Ken Schwaber created the five values of Scrum, the values are sequential. The correct sequence is Openness, Courage, Respect, Focus and Commitment. Jeff stated that Commitment is the lynchpin of Scrum.

Jeff explained the magic of commitment, by quoting W.H. Murray, leader of the Scottish Himalayan expedition. Murray said: "Until one is committed, there is hesitancy, the chance to draw back. Concerning all acts of initiative (and creation), there is one elementary truth, the ignorance of which kills countless ideas and splendid plans: that the moment one fully commits oneself, then Providence moves too. All sorts of things occur to help one that would never otherwise have never occurred. A whole stream of events issues from the decision, raising in one's favor all manner of unforeseen incidents and meetings and material assistance, which no man could have dreamed would have come his way. Whatever you can do, or dream you can do, begin it. Boldness has genius, power, and magic in it. Begin it now."

Once we commit, we will have focus to achieve our goals. Until then it was just a dream. Maybe serendipity is the result of commitment, maybe?

AUGUST 25

"It isn't that they can't see the solution. It is that they can't see the problem."

- G.K. Chesterton

I am sure that you have heard about a quote attributed to Albert Einstein – the quote goes "If I had only one hour to save the world, I would spend fifty-five minutes defining the problem, and only five minutes finding the solution." *(Note: there is no evidence that Einstein ever uttered the word. The quote is way too bombastic, and I am pretty sure that the person who uttered it, didn't understand the importance of working in iteration.)*

An agilist would probably say that "If I had only one hour to save the world, I would break them down into six ten minutes iterations, so that I will have six changes to save the world." Wrong attribution aside, the quote raised a very important notion that often time, it is not that we didn't know the right answer, we didn't know the right question to ask.

One of the most important tools in an agilist toolkit is the "5-Whys." I mentioned this briefly. This is a great tool to perform a root cause analysis. Asking why five times help you get to actual problem instead of just the symptoms. Taiichi Ohno, in his "Toyota Production System: Beyond Large Scale Producttion", gave an example:

1. *Why did the robot stop? The circuit overloaded, causing fuse to blow.*
2. *Why was the circuit overloaded? There was insufficient lube on the bearings, so they locked up.*
3. *Why was there insufficient lube on the bearings? The oil pump on the robot is not circulating enough oil.*
4. *Why was the pump not circulating enough oil? The pump intake is clogged with metal shavings.*
5. *Why was the intake clogged with metal shavings? Because there was no filter on the pump.*

AUGUST 26

A bug free software. Wouldn't it be nice. Maybe if we have all the time in the world to build software. Maybe if we have an infinite amount of time. But then if we have an infinite amount of time, we will have more fun observing a monkey creating the complete works of William Shakespeare. (This is known as the Infinite monkey theorem.). Alas, we don't have an infinite amount of time, we have until the end of the quarter if we are lucky, maybe the end of the sprint, if we are not. By the way, even if we have infinite time, I am willing to bet that some QA team members will still find some bug. It is fascinating to see QA work. The way they can think of how to use a product that no one in the right mind (or left mind, for that matter) would ever think of, in an infinite time.

So, there is always one more bug. This Lubarsky Law is not an excuse to do shoddy work. Being lean and agile means to do everything you can, when you need to do, to produce quality result without a single excess (no gold-plating. Gold-plating is when you deliver more than necessary. It is a form of waste. An over-processing waste.) Attention to quality and fitness for use are some of the most important attributes of great product.

Do you remember the joke that someone offers 3 kinds of services – Good, Cheap, Fast. But you can only pick 2. You can have Good & Cheap, but it won't be Fast. Or Fast and Good – it won't be Cheap though. Maybe Cheap and Fast – it's not going to be Good. Jeff Sutherland says that it is possible to have Good, Cheap and Fast using Scrum. We'll see.

AUGUST 27

"If a bug was addressed on the day it was created, it would take an hour to fix; three weeks later, it would take twenty-four hours. It didn't even matter if the bug was big or small, complicated or simple—it always took twenty-four times longer three weeks later."

- Jeff Sutherland

Jeff Sutherland told a story about his visit to the Palm in the early days of the internet (and Scrum). If you who are too young to remember dial up connection, rotary phones etc., Palm created Personal Digital Assistants (PDAs) – long before we have something called smart phones.

Palm was a data driven company (even at that time in the late nineties and early two-thousands) and the tracked everything they did. One of the things they track, and measure was how long it took to fix a bug. They analyzed how long it took to fix a bug if they did it right away as opposed to trying to fix it a few weeks later. Their findings show that on average, it took them twenty-four times longer to fix them bug if they wait. It didn't matter if the bug was complicated or simple. Doing it right the first time is very important. If you don't spend time to do it right the first time, you'll have to find time to do it over and it's going to be harder.

This is because as we are doing something (the developers writing codes) – we create a construct of all the related pieces. Once the work is "completed" we tear down the construct to make place for other work. When a developer is asked to fix a bug they introduced several weeks later, their brain has start from scratch, recreating the construct and it's much difficult to recreate the whole construct in a short time as opposed to construct that was scaffolded. It is easier to remember small pieces of information added incrementally as opposed to trying to remember everything all at once. This is also why I wrote this book this way without any coherent organization of topics. To allow your brain to scaffold.

AUGUST 28

"No matter how brilliant your mind or strategy, if you're playing a solo game, you'll always lose out to a team."
                                                    - Reid Hoffman

By all account, January 15th, 2009 was an ordinary day. The sun was out on that winter day when US Airways flight 1549 took off from LaGuardia airport, NY around 3:25 pm. It was headed to Charlotte, NC with 150 passengers and five crews.

About two minutes into the flight, the plane hit a flock of Canadian geese resulting in the damage of both engines. Attempt to restart the engine failed and Captain "Sully" Sullerberger decided to head to the airport. However, Sully decided that they couldn't reach an airport in time so Sully, with his crew, decided to land on the Hudson River, NY. This decision, dubbed as "The Miracle on the Hudson, saved the lives of all passengers and crew and made Sully a national hero.

In his keynote speech at the Cliff Lodge in Little Cottonwood Canyon, UT in 2017, Sully expressed his regret that he had become the face of miracle. He credited the success to his flight crew's teamwork to the success. Sully had been flying commercial airlines since the 80s and has been a proponent for a shift from an internal culture where pilots were "solo acts" to a culture of teamwork. Pilot was revered superior. Many co-pilots did not dare to speak against the pilot thus contributed to many early day airplane crashes. Since the change of the "cockpit culture" airline crews work together as a team. Sully wanted his flight attendants to be comfortable telling him any information and not to assume that he knew everything from the captain's seat at the nose of the plane. That teamwork, saved 155 lives that day.

AUGUST 29

"No one can whistle a symphony. It takes a whole orchestra to play it."

- H.E. Luccock

An orchestra is a large instrumental ensemble that combines instruments from different families. They may include strings, woodwinds, brass and percussions. Each of these families may have musical instruments such as violins, cellos, flute, oboe, trumpet, trombone, piano and even cymbal.

Teamwork is quite like an orchestra. Each team member plays their part, using their own skills and experience, contributing to the overall product. There are many roles that are like the conductor of the orchestra. A project manager's role is probably one of the ones most often compared to the conductor. Good project manager coordinates different people with different skillsets and guide them to deliver great product.

A project manager must manage the communication and interactions among team members, just as a conductor communicates with each musician to ensure their part is played in harmony with the rest of the orchestra. They must also monitor progress and address any issues that may arise, much like a conductor must monitor the performance and adjust tempo, volume, and phrasing on the fly to ensure a successful performance.

The audience plays a role of stakeholders, listening and enjoying the final product. It takes a combination of talent, hard work, and collaboration to produce a symphony, just like it takes a team of dedicated and skilled individuals to produce a successful project. Symphony and teamwork require coordination, communication, and cooperation to achieve a common goal and produce a successful outcome.

AUGUST 30

"No amount of observations of white swans can allow the inference that all swans are white, but the observation of a single black swan is sufficient to refute that conclusion."

- David Hume

Have you heard of a "turkey problem?" Nassim Nicholas Taleb, author of the book "the Black Swan" told it like this.

"Consider a turkey that is fed every day. Every single feeding will firm up the bird's belief that it is the general rule of life to be fed every day by friendly member of the human race "looking out for its best interests," as a politician would say. On the afternoon of the Wednesday before Thanksgiving, something *unexpected* will happen to the turkey. It will incur a revision of belief.

This metaphor illustrates the danger of overconfidence as well as the perils of empiricism. He said that there are traps built into any kind of knowledge gained from observation. The trap is illustrated clearly by the proceeding quote by David Hume.

Apparently, at some point in the past, people believed that all swans are white. A biologist documented his observation over a few years and thousands of swans, and they were all white. The question is how many observations is sufficient, how much data? And then someone found a black swan in Australia.

I hope this problem equip you with a certain sense of skepticism over some facts and be ready to recognize when you are almost ready to declare all swans are white.

AUGUST 31

"Nothing else in the world...not all the armies...is so powerful as an idea whose time has come."

- Victor Hugo

In John Wick: Chapter 4, after the bloodshed in Osaka, the Harbinger asked the Marquis de Gramont whether it was necessary. The Marquis responded with "This campaign is not to kill John Wick. It is to kill the idea of John Wick. And to do that, I must destroy everything that idea touches."

In our work we must consistently cultivate ideas. One of the powers of Scrum is that anyone can put anything in the product backlog (this is where Scrum keeps ideas for products.) Having enough contributions of ideas, there is a chance that we may have some great ideas. By understanding and harnessing the power of ideas, we can ensure our organizations stay ahead of the curve and create products that our customers will love.

One of the best examples of the idea that time has come is the invention of iPhone by Apple. The iPhone was an idea whose time had come. Its launch in 2007 was a turning point in the smartphone industry. Before the iPhone, smartphones were considered niche products for business professionals. Apple saw the potential for a consumer-focused smartphone and released the iPhone, which became an instant hit among consumers. The iPhone's innovation and design made it a cultural phenomenon, and its success has helped to shape the entire mobile market ever since.

SEPTEMBER

SEPTEMBER 1

"One of the most self-destructive tendencies within teams is to get so busy that we believe there's no time to get better at how we work."

- Aaron Dignan

I created a poster of the Agile Manifesto and it hangs in my office. On the poster I added a drawing of a cartoon that I saw.

In the cartoon, there were two cavemen hauling a wheelbarrow loaded with rocks. The wheelbarrow had square wheels. Needless to say, it looked like they were working very, very hard. On one side, stood another caveman. He was holding two round wheels and was offering them to the other cavemen. One caveman said "Sorry, we don't have time to try your wheels!" and the other caveman said "No thanks. We have been doing this since the stone age. We're good!"

This may sound like a bad joke, but I can tell you that it is not funny. There are many teams out there who are working very hard – really hard, and they are getting nowhere. Looking at teams like this, is like watching a hamster running very fast on a hamster wheel. It works hard but it doesn't go anywhere.

This is one of the main reasons that I consider retrospective as the most important event in Scrum. Retrospective is a mechanism to force you learn and become better at what you do. Every Sprint, your team get just a little bit better. Sprint over Sprint – these tiny improvements build up. The compounding effect to the improvement can mean the difference between merely surviving your competition, to thriving.

Retrospective is your competitive advantage. Ed D. would have probably pointed with his favorite Spiderman meme, "You know, I am something of a retrospective man myself!"

SEPTEMBER 2

"Only those who will risk going too far can possibly find out how far one can go."

- T.S. Eliot

Do you sometimes have crazy ideas and then you wise up and tell yourself that it was crazy idea and that's the end of the story? Here is the tale of someone who had a crazy idea and found out how far that crazy idea could go.

Dan Kwan, a director of the movie "Everything Everywhere All at Once" described the creation of the movie as: "So usually what happens is that the first idea is just the dumb idea. What's the silly, fun, stupid thing that makes us laugh? But we only pitch those things just to get a kick out of it. And then later down the line, if we're thinking about it still months or years later, it starts to attach itself to meaningful stories of our own, or philosophical ideas or things that feel therapeutic.... It's about the accumulation, that snowball effect that a single idea can have sometimes." – this "dumb idea," as of 2023 is the most awarded film of all time (including the Best Picture). Not bad for "dumb idea."

Did you watch it? [If you haven't SPOILER ALERT!]

Towards the end of the movie, it featured any crazy idea, a pet rock (with googly eyes). The Pet Rock was also a crazy idea. Gary Dahl created it as a joke because his friends were complaining about wanting a perfect pet that don't need feeding, walking, bathing, grooming, never gets sick or dies. He sold the pet rock for $4 each – in 1975 dollars – or $22 adjusted for inflation(the rock cost only one cent each) and sold about 1 million of them in less than a year. This crazy idea made Gary a millionaire. The movie may cause a resurgence of the pet rock craze. Crazy idea, eh?

SEPTEMBER 3

"Our greatest glory is not in never falling, but in rising every time we fall."

- Confucius

The Bible tells the story when a group of religious leaders who brought a woman accused of adultery to Jesus and demanded that Jesus determined her punishment. The Jewish law at stated that a woman caught in adultery should be stoned to death. In response to this demand Jesus challenged the mob and said, "He that is without sin among you, let him cast a stone at her." - John 8:7.

Failure is often treated as a bad thing – a demerit if you will. Companies often reward people who never makes mistakes. I would like to reframe the discussion a little bit. Now, there is a huge difference between someone who keep trying new things and fails, versus someone who stays at status quo and succeeds. Being incompetent at what you do is also another thing. At the rate of change today, staying where we are, maintaining a status quo, means that we are being left behind by our nimbler competitions. We need to keep moving and moving by breaking new grounds, trying new things, doings things that we have never done before. It also means that we will fail, often. And it is OK to fail. The score is not in the failing, it is in succeeding despite the fall.

The best example of this is the creation of new medicines. It could take up to a billion dollar to invent a new drug and the data show that only about 10% of drugs that reached clinical trial received FDA approval. 90% of their effort ends in expensive failures. But the ones that make it through, often, will be worth it. (Note: drug companies can bet big on these because they expect an exponential return on successful drugs – known as asymmetrical payoff.) So, try something new, bet big and bet wise

SEPTEMBER 4

"People don't change because you want them to change, people change when they're ready to change. So, understanding why, and when, and how people change is probably the biggest thing you can learn."

- Ron Quartel

For as long as I can remember, I've collected quotes. When I hear great lines in movies, TV shows, songs, books etc., I try to keep or remember them. Sometimes a quote sound good but I can't understand it. Sometimes, out of the blue, something that didn't make sense, suddenly hit me and things become very clear.

One of those quotes is "When the student is ready the teacher will appear. When the student is truly ready... The teacher will Disappear." from the Tao Te Ching. And then one day it suddenly become clear to me. I understand now that I was not ready to understand and that was why it never made sense. That is until it did.

Getting to people to change is the same. We cannot hold people by shoulder and shake them really hard or bombard them with data from analytics and the latest research result hoping they will change. You may find that, people who are opposed to the change you are proposing, are very much like the conspiracy theorists out there. The more you try to convince them to see it your way, the more they usually double-down on their original beliefs.

So, we can't really change people. The best we can do is to give them subtle nudges here and there. Showing them that a teeny tiny change is not a commitment, just trying something out. And little by little, they may convince themselves that they are the ones who change, because they want to, not because we want them to.

SEPTEMBER 5

"Remember, our goal is to minimize the amount we build (our output) and maximize the benefit we get from doing it (the outcomes and impact)."

- Jeff Patton

Elyahu Goldratt, in "Beyond the Goal" said that to win the most cherished prize in physics, the Noble Prize, there is only one simple criteria. "All you have to do is to publish only one article and this article can be only three or four pages. That's all. But the requirement is that when any other physicists read this article, their reaction is one and only one, and their reaction is "oh shit!" That's a Nobel Prize." It is the quality of the work and not the quantity of the work.

It would serve us well, in software development, to follow the same principle. To build a great product or software is not about how many lines of codes we produced, but it is more about what, our few lines of code can accomplish. It is not so much about the output but the outcome from our effective output.

Speaking of output and outcome, many are advising people to not focus on output and to focus on outcome instead. I would like to call BS to this nice sounding line. The fallacy is huge, but the fix is simple. The fallacy is in the thinking that output does not matter. Of course, it matters! It matters a great deal! Can you imagine when you are hungry (maybe even, hangry!) I tell you "Don't worry about eating or cooking something to eat, worry instead of being no longer hungry. You would probably throw a plate at me, if you have the energy to do so.

Having an expected outcome is dependent upon having the right output. So, you really need to focus on having the right (most effective and efficient) output, so that you will get the outcome that you need.

SEPTEMBER 6

"The sad reality is that despite all the talk about satisfying customer needs, there is very little understanding of what characteristics a customer need statement should possess and what structure, content, and syntax of a need statement should be."

- Anthony Ulwick

Listening to Clayton Christensen talked about the idea of the "Job to be Done" concept is quite an experience. He didn't come up with the concept, but he talked about it quite a lot. The concept was created by Anthony Ulwick, discussed in his book "What Customers Want."

Clayton said, in his TEDx Boston in July 2012: *"I have the characteristics: I'm unfortunately 60 years old now, I live in the suburbs, five children. Unfortunately, have all left and are living independently and life has become boring. But the fact that I have those characteristics doesn't cause me to go out and buy the New York Times. There might be a correlation between my characteristics and the propensity to buy the New York Times but the characteristics don't cause me to do anything. What causes us to do something is there's a job that arises in our life and we have to get the job done, and what causes us to buy a product or service is we have to reach out and find something that can do the job and pull it into our lives. That's the causal mechanism behind a purchase, is understanding what's the job. The insight there is that the customers is the wrong unit of analysis it's the job that we need to understand."*

This reminds us that our customers are not a set of demographics, characteristics or even hopes and dreams. Our customers have a very specific job to be done at very specific time. When the product that we are building can "do the job very well" at the time when it needs to be done, then our product will win out over our competitions.

SEPTEMBER 7

"Any fool can make things bigger, more complex, and more violent. It takes a touch of genius-and a lot of courage-to move in the opposite direction."

- E.F. Schumacher

At the palace of the kings of Phrygia in Gordium, in the 4th century BC, there was an elaborate knot tied to an ox-cart. The knot was made of several knots, all so tightly entangled that it was impossible to see how they were fastened. An oracle declared that any person who could unravel the Gordian knot, was destined to rule all of Asia.

When Alexander the Great arrived, he couldn't resist to try to untangle the knot. After trying without success for a time, Alexander stepped back from the knot and said, "It makes no difference how they are loosed." He then drew his sword and sliced the knot in half with a single stroke. True to the prophecy, Alexander went on to conquer Egypt and Asia.

Software that is made more complex than necessary is said to suffer from "Feature Creep." It happens when a product team continues adding features to the point that they undermine the product's value. Microsoft Word and Microsoft Excel are often cited as good software that have become bloated with feature creep. I uses some of the bloated Microsoft Word features to make this book and I used several of the bloated Microsoft Excel features to generate fancy reporting. While they may be useful for some advanced users, they can be overwhelming for users who just want so simple tools.

To avoid the trap of feature creep, keep the 80/20 Principle (or Pareto Principle) in mind. Know that 80% of your users only uses 20% of the Features to get some job done. Your job is to know which of those 20% features that are used and cultivate those.

SEPTEMBER 8

"Setting oneself on a predetermined course in unknown waters is the perfect way to sail straight into an iceberg."
- *Henry Mintzberg*

The Titanic, for lack of a better word, is titanic. Huge, enormous, very large. It had the reputation of and was designed to be unsinkable.

In 1912, the largest ship in the world (at that time) set sail from Southampton, England to New York. Although the ship was making good time, the captain was under some time pressure. At the end of day four, it was very cold. The sea's surface glimmered like glass making it hard for her crew to spot icebergs – which were common in the North Atlantic during that time of the year.

Despite the potential risk, the captain decided to go full speed ahead. By the time the ship lookout noticed an iceberg, the ship was too close to to maneuver around. The First Officer actually ordered the ship to go "full speed astern" to try to avoid the ice. He also closed the doors in the waterproof bulkheads. But there was more to the iceberg, hidden underneath the surface. Its underwater bulk punched holes into the Titanic's hull plates. Five days after it left port, the unsinkable ship, sank.

Agile framework's iterative process is designed to prevent the mistake of going full speed ahead into the unknown and avoiding conceptual icebergs. By releasing increment of functionalities every iteration, Agile teams are always adjusting to the customer's needs and wants. They break new ground by proceeding cautiously, adjusting their path as they go. They identify risks and potential pitfalls and take steps to mitigate every step of the way.

SEPTEMBER 9

"The greatest enemy of knowledge is not ignorance; it is the illusion of knowledge."

- Stephen Hawking

Once upon a time, there was a wise Zen master who lived on top of a mountain. (Do you realize that wise people always live far away from people, do they know something we don't?) People came from faraway lands to seek wisdom from the master.

One day, an eager scholar visited the master. The scholar said "Oh wise Zen master. I have learned from many great masters and all of them said that you are the wisest. I have come all way to ask you to teach me about Zen. Open my mind to enlightenment."

The Zen master smiled and said that they should talk over a cup of tea, so the master poured tea into the scholar's cup. He poured and poured and kept pouring even when the cup overflowed, and the hot tea started spilling over the scholar's robe. The scholar exclaimed. "Enough master. You have overflowed the cup. You are spilling the tea." The master stopped pouring and said to the scholar. "You, young master, are like this teacup, so full that nothing more can be added to it. Return when your cup is empty. I cannot teach you Zen unless you have emptied your cup first."

The dictionary defines "know-it-all" as one who claimed to know everything. People who think they know everything, won't be receptive to learning new knowledge. They can often be stubborn and occasionally be disruptive to progress. Watch out for the know-it-alls. Cultivate eager minds who are willing to profess ignorance and learn. And if Zen is not your thing – how about this advice from the Greek Stoic, Epictetus,"It is impossible for a man to learn what he thinks he already knows." – right, Jordan G?

SEPTEMBER 10

"If you tell people where to go, but not how to get there, you'll be amazed by the results."

- George S. Patton

Requirements – love them, hate them. Whether you are doing agile project management or "waterfall" project management, they are a fact of life in our world.

The Project Management Institute (PMI) used to call it "collect requirements" as if those requirements are just lying there – like over-ripe fallen apples, rotting under the tree (yes, this metaphor is intentional.) If you have tried to "gather" requirements before, they are not that easy (and IF they were that easy, just like the apples, you may want to check for signs of rot.) In real life, getting requirements is more like trying to pick a coconut from a very, very tall coconut tree (and you don't have any trained monkey to do it – yes, people trained monkeys to pick coconuts. Those monkeys are usually paid peanuts - well, maybe bananas!) Recently, the PMI changed the terminology from collecting/gathering to eliciting requirements. The term is used to signify that it takes some serious effort, and you often cannot be sure that you have all the requirements just by asking. Sometimes, you will have to do interviews, send questionnaires, observe users, do workshops, brainstorm, role plays and prototype.

In agile, we use customer's intent as a proxy for requirements. This is generally created in the form of a "Features, Advantages and Benefits" (FAB). An example of FAB for Slack software is:

Feature: Allows teams and team members to communicate via text messages, video calling, and audio huddles. Integrates with many different services like GSuite, GIPHY, and more.
Benefits: Streamlines communication between teams & keep comms all in one place, thus saving time.

SEPTEMBER 11

"I cannot say whether things will get better if we change; what I can say is that they must change if they are to get better."

- Georg Lichtenberg

The Organization and Change Management Consulting Market is projected to reach $1.97 billion by 2026. Helping people to change is a very lucrative business. This is probably because change, sustainable and long-lasting change, is hard.

Whenever people go through change, they go through several stages, known as the Change Curve. It consists of five stages:

1. Denial – we are in shock and our defense mechanism is up.
2. Anger – we lash out at the change or source of change.
3. Bargaining – we try to salvage the situation & offer compromise.
4. Depression – all hope is lost. Sadness and depression set in.
5. Acceptance – accept the change and adapt.

If you happen to realize that the change curve is very similar to the Kubler-Ross curve, better known as the Grief Curve, is that because it is. The reaction of most people, when encountering changes is very similar to their reaction when experiencing the loss of loved ones.

As much as we dislike it, change is inevitable. Every single moment of our live is marked by changing or being changed. When things are at status quo, they become stagnant and eventually wither. Now, not all changes are for the better, but if we want to have any chance at all to become better, change is our only path to get there.

SEPTEMBER 12

"The recipe of success is to study while others are sleeping, work while others are loafing, prepare while others are playing, and dream while others are wishing."
- William A. Ward

Many years ago, someone told me a great story. I remember the main point of the story but couldn't find the story on the internet. I am sure the story is out there if I have the right combination of keywords. So, I am going to attempt to retell the story.

A U.S. female paralympic champion (I don't remember who, when or even what sport) told a story of her success. She told of the time that she was practicing during Thanksgiving Holiday. She said that she was certain that all athletes that she competed against work very hard. They all posses great work ethic and they all worked out all the time. And then she said that she worked equally hard on Thanksgiving just in case her competitors, decided to skip this day, it being Thanksgiving holiday and all. And maybe, just maybe – this one extra practice was the only thing that differentiate her result with that of the competition. Success is the product of addition. I wouldn't be surprised if Cheryl W. told me that she also works out during Thanksgiving break. I am constantly amazed at how much dedication people have when doing something that matters.

Scrum is simple: The entire manual of Scrum - the Scrum Guide is only 13 pages long now (including the Table of Content). It outlines a set of basic practices. Remember that the practices are put there as forcing functions to build the right behavior over time. The authors suggest that we follow the practices consistently to slowly build the right behavior and mindset towards achieving agility.

SEPTEMBER 13

"We are too busy mopping the floor to turn off the faucet."

- Heard Somewhere

Murphy's Law states that "anything that can go wrong will go wrong." and a less eloquent person will just say, "shit happens." Right to the point. Shit happening is not news. It has been happening for as long as humanity has existed. Heck, if dinosaurs could talk, it happened to them too. The important lesson here is not that it happened. It is what we do after it happens.

Often, our first response, as *men of action* [my apology, I was going to use people of action, but it didn't have the same effect], is to do something, anything about it. We start fixing stuff. This is what we do, right? We have pain, we take pain medicine. We have a fever, we take fever reducer – we act.

When I used to work at a call center monitoring the health of internet connection for our clients, there was a site that most evenings, almost like clockwork, the circuit went down. We would send a dispatch technician to the site the next day and the problem would have resolved itself. This went on for months and we started to blame gremlins. One day, we got smart and decided to stake out the place. The field tech was very pleased even though that he had to work evening that day. He decided that if it was a gremlin, he was going to catch it. Alas, it wasn't a gremlin. No aliens playing a prank either. It turned out that the cleaning team went in every night (around the same time) and turned on the light in the closet. The power supply was cross wired with the light in the closet. When the closet light was turned off, the power supply to the router was turned off. So, valuable lessons learned. Get to the root cause and fix it and not just the symptoms.

SEPTEMBER 14

"Data is not information, information is not knowledge, knowledge is not understanding, understanding is not wisdom."

- Clifford Stoll

Once upon a time, the world was kind and simple and then things become more and more complex and now we live in primarily, a wicked world.

Robin M. Hogarth was a physician in the early 20th century New York to coin the term "kind" and "wicked" learning environment. "Kind" learning is marked by recurring patterns, where the situation is constrained. A game of chess is kind, golf (although I would really like to argue about this, but I know Robin was right) and baking a cake. In this environment, you get immediate feedback of what you did, and you can adjust. In a "wicked" environment, the feedback is delayed, infrequent. Sometimes feedback doesn't even exist or it's inaccurate. Learning from this could cause us to reinforce the wrong behavior.

I don't know if this is by design or coincidence, but the Wisdom Pyramid is spelled almost like wicked. There are (WIKD)
- Wisdom – applied – I better apply my brake and stop the car.
- Knowledge – context – the traffic light I am driving towards has turned red.
- Information – meaning – the south facing light on the corner on Main and 2nd has turned Red.
- Data – raw data – Red, #ff0000 | rgb(255,0,0)

Watch out for of "data driven" decision making in a wicked world. Please make sure that the "data" provides you with the right knowledge & wisdom.

SEPTEMBER 15

"There is one thing I've learned in 52 years of public service is that there is no problem so complex, nor crisis so grave that it cannot be satisfactorily resolved within 20 minutes."

- Winston Churchill

The term "analysis paralysis" means an inability to make decision caused by over- thinking a problem. One of the reasons for this phenomenon could be because we have too much data or too many options. People with analysis paralysis often waste time, energy and resources. Going back and forth without deciding.

I am guessing that Sir Winston Churchill might have been exaggerating a little bit when he said, "satisfactorily resolved within 20 minutes." but he may not be too far off. Recall our discussion about the Gordian Knot. How it was almost impossible to untangle and Alexander the Great, once he decided on the right course of action, resolved the problem with a swing of his blade.

In Scrum, the daily stand up is timeboxed at 15 minutes. 15-minutes in not a lot of time to plan, coordinate and resolve blockers. But it is doable. We just need to focus on the most important matter at hands and evaluate and make decisions. Few things we do at work are a matter of life and death. If it turned out that our first decision was not optimal, we can learn from it and iterate. This is one of the main reasons why being able to learn is a key component from iterative effort.

Speaking of life and death and focus, here's a little gallows humor gem, "when a man knows he is to be hanged in a fortnight, it concentrates his mind wonderfully. – William Dodd"

SEPTEMBER 16

"Without a goal, discipline is nothing but self-punishment."

- Auliq Ice

The term "Sisyphean" means pointless or interminable activities. The term originated from Sisyphus. He was a character in Greek mythology who was punished to push a heavy (and enchanted) boulder up a steep hill only to have it roll back down every time he almost reaches the top (that's the enchantment.)

I am tempted to edit the preceding quote as "without an **achievable** goal, discipline is nothing but self-punishment." Having discipline is great. People with discipline can accomplish (almost) anything. Take, for example, the discipline of this old man. He was 90 years old, and he lived near Taihang and Wangwu mountains in the Yu province in China. The position of the mountain was an inconvenience, so he decided to move the mountain. So, he started digging with a hoe and a basket and started piling the dirt. People laughed at him and at the impossibility of the task, thus he was named the "Foolish Old Man." When people asked what he was expecting to do because there was no way he could have finished the work, as disciplined as he was, in his lifetime. The old man said that he may not finish his task in his lifetime, but through his own and his descendants' hard work, someday the mountain will be moved. The gods in heaven took pity of the old man and separated the mountains.

Unfortunately (or fortunately) we cannot rely on divine intervention to make our lives harder or easier. We have to rely on ourselves to set smart and achievable goals that will make our days at work and life a meaningful and give us Purpose, Autonomy and Mastery. When we have that, we can apply a directed discipline to accomplishing the goal. Even if you could, would you, should you try to move a mountain?

SEPTEMBER 17

"The best time to plant a tree was 20 years ago, and the next best time is today."

- Chinese Proverb

When we look back at the decisions we have made in our work, or life, we often find that we could have done so much better. Retrospective is a very powerful thing to have. In agile, we conduct retrospective, postmortem, or RCA (Root Cause Analysis) activities to help us become better. It is a very important mechanism to foster continuous improvement mindset. One of our team members, Tobin B. is major believer in running great retrospectives. He is always gung-ho in running many of the agile events. SOS, checked. Retrospective, checked!

Used incorrectly, however, it can also be paralyzing. It may cause us to start questioning our decision-making abilities. It is never comfortable to look back honestly to the past and occasionally see "who" messed up. Our goal is not to point fingers or to find a scape goat. Our goal is not to figure out the "who". Our goal is to find the "what". What went wrong. Once we have identified what went wrong, we can start to do something to prevent it from happening again.

Don't allow those "should-haves", "could-haves" or "would-haves" ruin your ability to learn from the past poor decisions. Instead, know that in the grand scheme of things, everyone will make mistakes. They key to growth is to learn from them today and grow for a better tomorrow. Instead of lamenting the fact that we should have planted a tree 20 years ago, start now. Carpe diem!

SEPTEMBER 18

"If I had asked people what they wanted, they would have said faster horses."

- Henry Ford

First of all, there is no evidence that Henry Ford actually said that. He was, however, known to have put great importance in understanding the customers preferences. Note that there is a huge difference between understanding customer preferences to blindly listening to customers.

We are, in no small part, made up of our biases. Often, we are driven by some of our unconscious bias that shapes our thoughts, behaviors and actions. Therefore, we don't know what we don't know. Just like, sometimes, our stakeholders may not really know what they want. Worse yet, sometimes they "think" they know what they want.

Take the famous Pepsi Challenge for example. In the late 1970s Pepsi conducted a series blind taste test. People were asked to taste two cups of soft drink. One containing Coca Cola and the other Pepsi Cola. The test showed that people preferred Pepsi over Coca Cola. This is an example of what is known as Choice Modelling. Choice Modelling attempts to tease out people's revealed preferences (what you really like when no one is looking) over their stated preferences (what you say you like when someone ask.)

Although Choice Modelling is a powerful tool, like any tools, we need to use it with caution. Because, in Dan Ariely's word – people are predictably irrational (his book is titled "Predictably Irrational). Many of our behaviors are misguided. Individually, we seldom do things in absolute. Of course, in the grand scheme of things, according to the law of large numbers, we are more similar that different. However, individually, we are still unique. Understanding the difference, is key.

SEPTEMBER 19

"If you adopt only one agile practice, let it be retrospectives. Everything else will follow."

- Woody Zuill

We talked a lot of retrospectives. I am sure, by now, you have heard me saying that Sprint Retrospective is the most important event in Scrum. And it is not just in Scrum. In all agile practices (yes, that includes Kanban too.) This practice is so important, I feel compelled to say it again and again. "If you don't do retrospectives, there is no reason for you to do agile!"

Many have asked about the rest of the Scrum events, especially Sprint Planning. Surely planning has got to be the most important practice. Heck, we talked about planning as often, if not more, than retrospective. Let's run through a scenario. You have just started an important project. Being "men of action", you took the plunge and started working. Things didn't turn out as well as you expected so you perform **Retrospective**. Maybe the result of the retrospective said that you need to plan the work instead of just taking the plunge. You have just invented (Sprint) **Planning**. You planned your work, things got better. But you weren't sure how much to future you should plan. During next retrospective, you agree to plan only for two weeks. And you have just invented the **Sprint**. You worked in a specific cadence (Sprint) and you Planned well, but feel like waiting for two weeks to get together is too long, some things may need to be replanned, you decided to do some quick daily check-ins to make sure that the plans are still sound. Well, you have just invented the **Daily Scrum**. Next you may think that you need a mechanism to review the result of your work during the sprint and the **Sprint Review** is born. You also decided that you need to improve the way you tee up work, Backlog and Backlog Refinement is born.

You've got the idea.

SEPTEMBER 20

"No goal, regardless of how small can be achieved without adequate training."

- Taiichi Ohno

The article "2 Mental Abilities Separate Humans from Animals" in Scientific American start with a thought provoking question, "Why are we, and not the gorillas, running the zoos?"

Even though humans are some of the weakest mammals on the planet, as of the writing of this book, we dominate other, often much stronger, species. At least until AI (read: Skynet) takes over.

The 2 mental abilities are:

1. Our ability to run scenarios to envision and mentally consider many possible situations and anticipate different outcomes.
2. Our drive to exchange our thoughts with others.

Simply put, we are capable of a leap of logic, and we are capable of teaching & learning.

Training is an essential part of any learning organization. We have established that maintaining status quo is the surest path to extinction. To thrive, our organization needs to continue to learn and share the result of those learnings throughout the company. We should aim to train and equip our people so that they are so good at what they do, they can leave and work elsewhere anytime they want. And, equally important, that we treat them in such way, that they choose to stay and grow with us instead. Henry Ford said that "The only thing worse than training your employees and having them leave is not training them and having them stay."

SEPTEMBER 21

"In any given moment we have two options: to step forward into growth or to step back into safety."

- Abraham Maslow

We have established the fact that, whether we like it or not "shit happens." As a matter of fact, it has been happening long before we existed, and it will continue to happen after we are gone. The important thing is not that shit happens, but what do we do after it happens.

Bad things happened to good people. You and I are definitely good people, and we definitely *don't deserve* this bad thing – we can curse the sky and lament our bad luck. Some may start thinking that it is just the way it is. Once we have started believing that we have no agency over what happens to us, we may fall into a sense of despair. The term for this condition is learned helplessness. An alternative to learned helplessness is having a Sense of Agency. When we make decisions or take actions, we feel that we are on the driver's seat. We don't feel as if things simply happen. When something happens to people with a strong sense of agency, they learned from their actions and results and they decide to do better, to improve.

This is the sense that we are building every sprint by performing retrospectives. We looked at what happened, good or bad, and decide to continue doing the good things and mitigate or fix the bad thing. Good retrospectives do not involve lamenting about the things that we couldn't change, like "the system" and rather focus on the things that we have control over. If everyone is doing it, collectively, we can improve "the system." We are, after all, part of "the system."

Note. A study in nursing homes have shown that people with sense of control (agency) lives longer that people who don't feel that they have any choices.

SEPTEMBER 22

"Winning is not a "sometimes" thing. You don't win once in a awhile, you don't do things right once in a while, you do them right all of the time. Winning is a habit, unfortunately, so is losing."

- Vince Lombardi

In the book "The Power of Habit", Charles Duhigg talks about the science of habit and how habit can transform lives, organizations and societies. Winning is a habit, and losing is a habit. Excellence is a habit. Agility is also a habit. Habits are more powerful than will, motivation, or even inspiration, because when a habit is established, it doesn't require any of those other things anymore.

Scrum helps build good habit I am guilty of talking about Scrum while I talk about agile. Agile is not Scrum. There are many frameworks and practices out there that are agile including Kanban and Extreme Programming. I use Scrum because it is the most ubiquitous framework. Scrum is simple. Many of the Scrum practices are designed as forcing functions to build the right habit. Think of Scrum as a tricycle. The more you understand the intent of each of Scrums practices, the closer you are to being agile.

For example, the Daily Scrum helps build the habit of having regular communication and collaboration. Sprint Planning build the habit of organization and purposeful and goal orientated work. Sprint Review and Retrospective build the habit of continuous improvement, achievement and innovation.

In short, Scrum events build habits by providing structured opportunities for collaboration, communication, planning and learning.

SEPTEMBER 23

"People don't want a quarter inch drill. They want a quarter in hole."

- Theodore Levitt

We talked about the importance of having a lot of ideas in order to increase the odds of coming up with the "right" ideas. We then validate each idea very rapidly and discard the ones that don't work. Anthony Ulwick, the creator of the Job to Be Done (JTBD) framework explained that it was the wrong approach. This brute force approach is too slow, too time consuming, too expensive with very minimal chance of us getting lucky. It is akin to hitting the jackpot in a slot machine. Although people do hit jackpots in slot machine the house always wins.

Ulwick proposed that innovation or product development should really start by identifying the unmet needs of jobs that our customers want done. He created a formula to define what a market is. Market is defined as the job executor plus the job to be done. He further elaborated the core job that customer needs to be done is described using verb + objective of the vert + contextual clarifier. An example would be *"as a handyman, I want to cut a piece of wood in a straight line."*

When you read that example, what does that remind you of? Yes. It is almost identical with the User Story template – *As a* [**who** wants to do something], *I want* [**what** do they want to do], *so that* [**why** do they want to do it] – the only difference is that we added the reasons why someone want to do the job. The why is not always required. *So that I will make a straight cut* is implied with the job.

Ulwick's method makes a lot of sense. To learn more about it, go read his book call "Job to Be Done", it's a fascinating read.

SEPTEMBER 24

"The important thing is not your process. The important thing is your process for improving your process."

- Henrik Kniberg

Process is one of those words that, when uttered, invites groans and frustrations. Aren't we supposed to be doing agile? And aren't processes anti agile? It said so in the Agile Manifesto that reads *"Individual Interaction Over Processes and Tools"* – see, processes and tools are bad for agile, right? Nope!

How important is having good process? W. Edwards Deming has this to say, "If you can't describe what you are doing as a process, you don't know what you're doing." Lisa Gonzalez and Mike Patton in their book "Process: How Discipline and Consistence Will Set You and Your Business Free" explained that ***all humans*** – even the most innovative – are naturally and instinctively process oriented. The survival of our species can be credited to adaptive process. They learned to stop doing deadly things (eating poisonous berries, getting eaten by sabretooth tiger) and continue doing what kept them alive (banding together, living in protected caves). They passed on everything they learned to us and thus the "process" of living became less stressful. Did you notice that even our ancestors supposedly had a process of improving their processes to survive – it sounded like they were doing ***retrospectives*** didn't they? – mind-blown!

One final note, here is a statement that I like from one of Clayton Christensen's books – "The Prosperity Paradox" Clay wrote: "At the outset, an organization survives because of its resources. But an organization thrives in the long term because of its processes." It is a process to get there. As Kit B., is fond of saying, "The best way of working is yet to be discovered!" *[Here's looking at you, Kit!]*

SEPTEMBER 25

> *"Inspection to improve quality is too late, ineffective, costly. Quality comes not from inspection, but from the improvement of the production process."*
>
> *- W. Edwards Deming*

When do you test the feature that you have just built? If you are like most teams, you have them tested after you have done coding and has officially passed on the responsibility to the Quality Assurance (QA) team.

QA then do their magic – perform some mindbogglingly unpredictable way to use the feature. They either put their seal of approval or they find a problem and kicked the work back to you as bug(s).

In his book "Smarter Faster Better", Charles Duhigg explained how General Motors used to inspect quality and handle defect. *"At GM, all that really mattered was keeping production on pace. Employees sometimes discovered mistakes on cars as they moved along the conveyor belt, but rather than stop and fix the problems, they would mark the vehicle with a wax crayon or a Post-it note and let it continue on its way. Eventually, those fully assembled autos would be hauled into the back lot and taken apart to repair the error."*

As a contrast, at Toyota, everyone knows that they are responsible for the quality. At Toyota Manufacturing plant, whenever an error was discovered, the worker would pull a hanging cable, called an Andon cord (they were all over the plant), and stopped the line so that they can fix the problem there and then. This solution of shifting left promoted the improvement of the production process and not the fixing of errors at the end of the line. Ask me about an interesting incident involving the President of Toyota, a guy named Joe and the Andon cord.

SEPTEMBER 26

"Every strike brings me closer to the next home run."
- Babe Ruth

In my case, while writing this book, I could probably say that "Every keystroke brings me closer to the next book." I know that at this moment, I only have a few more pages to write and I find myself giddy with the anticipation. When I started this book, I had a set of goals and now that I am here, when I can almost see the end point, I feel my heart beat a little faster and I am brimming with energy.

Having a clear and achievable goal is very important. It is important not because Scrum tells you that you must have a Sprint goal. Not because all agile frameworks try to tell us that it is important. It is important because of what we are as humans.

In "Leaders Eat Last", Simon Sinek explained that evolution have made us all addicts. Our brains supply us with many chemicals to drive us towards certain habits that would ensure our survival. The chemical endorphins and dopamine are the ones that drive us to achieve our goals.

He told a story of the time of our Paleolithic ancestor. As hunter and gatherers, they spent most of their existence in the search of food. Their brains (and ours too because we inherited the latest iteration of their evolution) supplied them with endorphins for endurance to go far away in search of food. When our ancestor saw a good food source, they got hit by a dose of dopamine to incentivize them to stay focused on the task. When they make progress, they got more dopamine until they reached the goal and bam! They were rewarded by a big hit of dopamine. Dopamine gives us an incentive for progress. This is one of the main reasons why it is a good idea for agile team members to move their own tickets on the kanban board towards Done. Doing so, they will be rewarded by dopamine so that they will continue to strive for Done.

SEPTEMBER 27

"Story point estimation establishes the gap of understanding."

- This Yoda

Here is another recurring theme, the point of doing story point estimation is not to have story points. The resulting story point is the byproduct of the process that help you obtain understanding of the job to be done. Once the discussion has been completed and differing point of views are considered, it no longer really matters if you estimate using modified Fibonacci (1,2,3,5,8,13,20, 40, 100) or Lady Finger banana, Cavendish banana, Plantain banana (for the non-banana-aficionados Lady Finger banana is small, Cavendish is medium and Plaintain is large), or sands, pebbles, rocks. (I made the banana and rock estimation up – just to illustrate a point that it doesn't matter what method you use.)

Working on coming up with story point estimation, helps you establish or identify the gaps in understanding (or misunderstanding for that matter.) Let's pretend that the team use the planning poker technique to come up with an estimation. In Scrum, the Product Owner read the user story, the team asks clarifying questions to gain understanding of the intent of the story, discusses and even propose changes (if necessary) and once everyone has expressed their understanding, they are ready to estimate. They do so by individually selecting a card that has one of the points. Once everyone has estimated, the numbers are revealed. If the numbers come up with 2,2,5,3,2,5,3 – that means that the gap of understanding is small – the estimate is 2,3 or 5. There is only one number between 2 and 5. The gap of understanding is small. The team can pick the median or highest number and move on. If the estimate is 1,1,5,3,2,5,3 – now the gap of understanding is larger – there are 2 numbers between 1 and 5. At this point, it is important to discuss to understand what may have caused the gap. Remember to keep it simple. It's all just an estimate any way. You don't need to contest every single story point.

SEPTEMBER 28

"It doesn't matter what you say you believe – it only matters what you do."

- Robert Fulghum

There was an old story about the time the Buddha was tested by his rival Mara (in Buddhism, Mara is personification of death and desire – the bad guy).

The news that the Buddha was visiting and giving his sermon was all over the town. It was customary to offer an old lamp to show devotion and appreciation. Everyone in the town was buying oil and oil lamps. There was an old woman who really wanted to attend the sermon. She tried to beg for alms but couldn't find anyone to give her the money to buy the oil. She tried to beg the oil merchant for just a little bit of oil, but she was refused. She had nothing that the merchant wanted. The old woman didn't have anything of value. Except that she had long beautiful hair so the merchant said, "I can trade a little bit of oil for your hair." The woman was overjoyed. She was proud of her – it was her most only possession, but she was happy that she could finally show her devotion to the Buddha. While everyone was jockeying for prime position to show their stature, the old woman was able to put her lamp on the lowest position. During the sermon, Mara came and blew all the oil lamps away. All lamp was extinguished except for one – the one from the old woman. The Buddha realized the importance of that lamp and told Mara "If you were to pour the water from all the oceans over this lamp, it still wouldn't go out. The water in all the rivers and the lakes of the world could not extinguish it. Why not? Because this lamp was offered with devotion and with purity of heart and mind." Mara tried and tried but failed and left the congregation alone.

This story shows that what you do, despite all challenges means more than what you say you believe.

SEPTEMBER 29

"You have to find something that you love enough to be able to take risks, jump over the hurdles and break though the brick walls that are always going to be placed in front of you. If you don't have that kind of feeling for what it is you are doing, you'll stop at the first giant hurdle."

- George Lucas

What motivates you? Are you motivated by more money, more responsibilities or more fulfillment?

There are many theories about motivation and job satisfaction, but I would like to talk about Herzberg's Motivation-Hygiene Theory. Herzberg observed a common assumption that job satisfaction exists in one big continuum – starting with very happy on one side to absolutely miserable on the other. He stated that job satisfaction and dissatisfaction exist on two different planes, each with its own set of factors. One plane is called the hygiene factors – this contains elements that, if not done right, will cause us to be dissatisfied. They include status, salary, job security, company policies and how our boss treats us. The best you can do with hygiene factors is to get it right. Getting it wrong will cause immediate dissatisfaction and getting it right will only yield the absence of dissatisfaction. There is no upside on getting this right but plenty of downside when getting it wrong. The other side is called motivation factors. They include challenge, recognition, responsibility and personal growth. If we feel like we are making meaningful contribution, we will feel motivated. This is also called intrinsic motivation.

This shows that we are truly complex being and we seldom just one thing or another. It is seldom black or white. Our actions are seldom binaries.

SEPTEMBER 30

"Human beings, who are almost unique in having the ability to learn from the experience of others, are also remarkable for their apparent disinclination to do so."

- Douglas Adams

In answering the question "Why are we, and not the gorillas, running the zoos?" we know that one of the key reasons is about ability to learn and pass on our processes of survival. Life has been good for us, human. Especially you and me. If you are reading this book, the threat of survival is no longer front and center in our life. We have other, more pressing, world altering matters to attend to such as thinking about what features to build and what's for lunch – fish tacos anyone?

We possess another interesting characteristic, pointed out by Douglas Adams, that is sometimes, we do not learn. Our world is littered by examples where we are doomed by our inabilities to learn from the past. The Great Depression of the 1930s was repeated in the 2008 Global Financial Crisis. The Covid-19 Global Pandemic is another example. despite the many pandemics that we have survived, we were caught unprepared by the rapid growth of the disease.

I am sure you know what I am going to say next. Yes, you are right. This is one of main reasons why Retrospective is the most important event that we must do consistently. It is our avenue for learning, for getting better. If we are not learning, there is no reason for us to work in iteration. If we are not learning, there is no reason to try to be agile.

Let's go build a learning organization because, we do give a shit! I am sure Mike B, a.k.a. the Bern would give us a thumbs up and will share one of his timely Dad jokes.

THE END?

Where is the rest of the book? The year does not end on September 30th. Do you know something that we don't? Is the world finally ending and Nostradamus was right all along?

Well, hold your horses, partner! The reason is less sinister than that.

I end the book here because this book is intended to be part one of a four-part series. Each quarter, when you attend the quarterly planning, you will get an installment of the book.

This is also created in the spirit of building an MVP. I don't know if I could pull it off and I don't know if, after this book is printed and distributed, it will have the reactions or results that I expect. One of the ways to test my hypothesis is to build an MVP and get feedback.

That's why this last page is aptly titled "The End?" with a question mark. Whether it ends or not, is really, up to you. If you like it and see the value in this, please let me know. If you think that there is something that could have been improved, let me know. If you truly hate this and can't wait to burn this book, go ahead and do it – just don't tell me about it.

So, maybe we will have another dose of nourishment or not. Only time will tell. In the meantime, please continue your journey of self-betterment. Only **YOU** can do it for you. Because it is only "when the students are ready, the teacher will appear!"

On a final note, here is a timeless advise from Jess H. "keep calm and game on!"

Out of the building, Yoda is! hmmm.

APPENDIX

What is Agile?

Agile is an iterative approach to project management and software development that helps teams deliver value to their customers faster.

In the 1990s, responding to the many challenges of waterfall processes, some lighter-weight and more iterative development methods arose. In 2001, many of the leaders (later known as "the snowbird 17") of these frameworks came together in Snowbird, Utah. While there were differences of opinion on the specific merits of one method over another, the attendees agreed that their shared values and beliefs dwarfed the differences. The result was a Manifesto for Agile Software Development, a turning point that clarified the new approach and started to bring the benefits of these innovative methods to the whole development industry.

It was that Agile Manifesto that kick-started our processes. It's important that organizations understand and embrace all of this.

After completing the Agile Manifesto, the Snowbird 17 continued to refine the thoughts and principles behind the four values and after some back and forth, they expanded on the handful of sentences that make up the value. These are known as the Twelve Principles of Agile Software Since then, the Agile Manifesto has changed minimally, if at all. But the world surrounding agile couldn't be more different.

You will notice that the principles use the term "software" often, it is because, it was originally intended to solve a software development problem. A lot has changed since and the idea of agility is no longer confined to the world of software. To help you adapt the values and principles to your need, all you need to do is to replace the word "software" to "system" or "solutions" and suddenly it is relevant again.

Manifesto for Agile Software Development

We are uncovering better ways of developing
software by doing it and helping others do it.
Through this work we have come to value:

Individuals and interactions over processes and tools
Working software over comprehensive documentation
Customer collaboration over contract negotiation
Responding to change over following a plan

That is, while there is value in the items on the right,
we value the items on the left more.

Kent Beck	James Grenning	Robert C. Martin
Mike Beedle	Jim Highsmith	Steve Mellor
Arie van Bennekum	Andrew Hunt	Ken Schwaber
Alistair Cockburn	Ron Jeffries	Jeff Sutherland
Ward Cunningham	Jon Kern	Dave Thomas
Martin Fowler		Brian Marick

Principles behind the Agile Manifesto
We follow these principles:

1. Our highest priority is to satisfy the customer through early and continuous delivery of valuable software.
2. Welcome changing requirements, even late in development. Agile processes harness change for the customer's competitive advantage.
3. Deliver working software frequently, from a couple of weeks to a couple of months, with a preference to the shorter timescale.
4. Business people and developers must work together daily throughout the project.
5. Build projects around motivated individuals. Give them the environment and support they need and trust them to get the job done.
6. The most efficient and effective method of conveying information to and within a development team is face-to-face conversation.
7. Working software is the primary measure of progress.
8. Agile processes promote sustainable development. The sponsors, developers, and users should be able to maintain a constant pace indefinitely.
9. Continuous attention to technical excellence and good design enhances agility.
10. Simplicity--the art of maximizing the amount of work not done--is essential.
11. The best architectures, requirements, and designs emerge from self-organizing teams.
12. At regular intervals, the team reflects on how to become more effective, then tunes and adjusts its behavior accordingly.

EVERYTHING YOU NEED TO KNOW ABOUT SCRUM⁺

TERMINOLOGY

PRODUCT BACKLOG
An emergent, ordered list of User Stories needed to build or improve a product.
Product Backlog represents opportunity NOT commitment.

SPRINT BACKLOG
Selected list of User Stories from the Product Backlog that the Scrum team plan to finish within the Sprint. Items in the Sprint Backlog should be completed within a Sprint.

SPRINT / ITERATION
Scrum iterations are called Sprints. Sprint could be as short as one week and as long as four weeks. At 2K we have a synchronized cadence of two weeks - starting on Wednesday, ending on Tuesday.

EPICS
A large body of work of large User Stories that needs to decomposed in smaller set of User Stories. In a team environment, the term Epics is often interchangeable with "Features".

USER STORIES
Short description of functionality written in the perspective of a user. "as a [user], I want to [do something], so that [benefit]".
User Stories should be completed within a Sprint & is related to an Epic.

ACCEPTANCE CRITERIA
A list of functionalities or conditions that must be satisfied because the work can be considered "DONE". Generally written in the "Given, When, Then" format. It could also be written in a "verify that" format.

DEFINITION OF DONE
A list of criteria that must be satisfied because a User Story or Epic can be considered "DONE". The criteria may varies from team to team, depending on the team's capability to release their work to production.

VELOCITY
Total number of story points that the team completed within a Sprint. To be used when planning on how much the team can complete in the upcoming Sprints. It is better to use the average of the last 3 Sprints.

BURNDOWN CHART
A metric showing the team's burn-rate - how much work the team had completed on daily basis within a Sprint, comparing how much work the team has at the the start of the Sprint

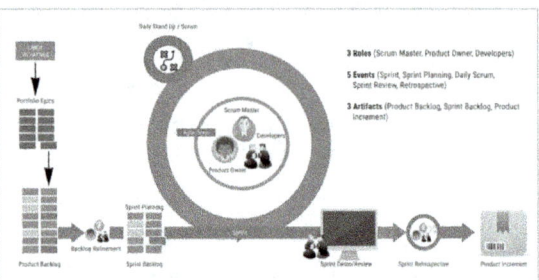

3 **Roles** (Scrum Master, Product Owner, Developers)

5 **Events** (Sprint, Sprint Planning, Daily Scrum, Sprint Review, Retrospective)

3 **Artifacts** (Product Backlog, Sprint Backlog, Product Increment)

EVENTS

1. **JAD (JOINT APPLICATION DESIGN)*** - Ad Hoc meeting between Design, Engineering and Product to breakdown Epic or Feature into a list of User Stories that when completed, satisfy the acceptance criteria the Epic/Feature
2. **BACKLOG REFINEMENT** - One to two hours per week. Discuss Users Stories in Product Backlog. Put Story Point (in modified Fibonacci - 1,2,3,5,8,13,20,40, 80, 100) to signify full understanding of the intent of the User Story.
3. **SPRINT PLANNING** - One to two hour per Sprint. Select a list of User Stories (that have Story Point) that the team plan to complete in the upcoming Sprint. Stop until the total story reaches +/-10% of the team average Velocity.
4. **DAILY STAND-UP** - 15 minutes daily (may be followed by a meet after). The team synchronize their activities, create a day plan, ask and provide help.
5. **SPRINT REVIEW / DEMO** - One hour per Sprint on the last day of the Sprint. The team review how the Sprint went and demonstrate the result of the work.
6. **SPRINT RETROSPECTIVE** - One hour per Sprint on the last day of the Sprint. The team discuss the result of the Sprint. Review some quantitative metrics and qualitative metric. Select one or two items of improvement and work on improving in the upcoming Sprint.

SCRUM ROLES

PRODUCT OWNER	SCRUM MASTER	AGILE TEAM
Work with stakeholders to come up with solutions to customers' problem.	Coach the team in Scrum and agile practices. Help facilitate scrum events.	Cross functional group of people (that include Design, Developers, QA and other specialty skills, that self organizes to the meet the Sprint goals.
If there is no Product Owner in the team, The role of the Product Owner will be played by a **PRODUCT MANAGER.**	If there is no Scrum Master The role of the Scrum Master can be played by an **ENGINEERING MANAGER/LEAD or DEV**	The team collaborate to deliver an increment of value every Sprint.

*SCRUM+ because not everything you see here are in accordance to the Scrum Guide 2020